The Geometry and Features of Tone

Summer Institute of Linguistics and
The University of Texas at Arlington
Publications in Linguistics

Publication 133

Publications in Linguistics is a series published jointly by the Summer Institute of Linguistics and The University of Texas at Arlington. The series is a venue for works covering a broad range of topics in linguistics especially the analytical treatment of minority languages from all parts of the world. While most volumes are authored by members of the Institute, suitable works by others will also form part of the series.

Series Editor

Mildred L. Larson, Summer Institute of Linguistics
Donald A. Burquest, University of Texas at Arlington

Volume Editor

Bonnie Brown

Production Staff

Bonnie Brown, Managing Editor
Laurie Nelson, Production Manager
Judy Benjamin, Compositor
Hazel Shorey, Graphic Artist

The Geometry and Features of Tone

Keith Snider

A Publication of
The Summer Institute of Linguistics
and
The University of Texas at Arlington

©1999 by the Summer Institute of Linguistics, Inc.
Library of Congress Catalog No: 99-61562
ISBN: 1-55671-077-1
ISSN: 1040-0850

Printed in the United States of America
All Rights Reserved

09 08 07 06 05 04 03 02 01 00 10 9 8 7 6 5 4 3 2 1

Copies of this and other publications of the Summer Institute of Linguistics may be obtained from

International Academic Bookstore
Summer Institute of Linguistics
7500 W. Camp Wisdom Rd.
Dallas TX 75236-5699

Voice: 972-708-7404
Fax: 972-708-7433
Email: academic_books@sil.org
Internet:http://www.sil.org

Contents

Contents

Abbreviations

AM	associative marker
ATR	Advanced Tongue Root
BD	Bamileke-Dschang
BT	boundary tone
CONT	continuous
FLD	Final *l*-Docking
Hi	High tone
HAB	habitual
HTS	Hi Tone Spread
LHS	Lexcal *h*-Spread
Lo	Low tone
NC	Noun class
NEG	negativizer
OCP	Obligatory Contour Principle
OT	Optimal Theory
P	plural
PDFA	Postlexical Default Feature Assignment
PHS	Postlexical Hi-Spread
S	singular
SPEC	specifier
RTT	Register Tier Theory
TBU	tone-bearing unit
TRN	Tonal Root Node

Preface

> It is God's privilege to conceal
> things and the king's privilege
> to discover them. (Proverbs
> 25:2, *Holy Bible*, New Living
> Translation)

The Geometry and Features of Tone presents a model for the phonological representation of tone—what features are involved, how they relate to tone-bearing units (TBUs), and how they interact with one another. The model it presents, REGISTER TIER THEORY, is not a general theory of phonology. Instead, being a theory of phonological features, it is integrated into the broader theories of lexical phonology, autosegmental phonology, and optimality theory, where it replaces the single-tier representations for tone that tend to dominate the literature.

What must a model for the phonological representation of tone be able to do? First and foremost, it needs to be able to uniquely represent each tone phoneme in any given language. Just as a model for vocalic phenomena must be able to distinguish the phoneme /o/ from the phonemes /e/ and /i/, so a model for tonal phenomena must be able to distinguish the tone phoneme High (Hi) from the tone phonemes Mid and Low (Lo). It is not enough, however, just to be able to distinguish one phoneme from

I wish to thank Tyndale House Publishers Inc., Wheaton, Illinois 60189, U.S.A. for permission to quote Proverbs 25:2 from the *Holy Bible*, New Living Translation. All rights reserved.

another. Phonemes group together in natural classes so that in certain environments the phonological behavior of /e/, for example, might pattern after that of /o/, while in certain other environments it might pattern after that of /i/. A good model captures these similarities by assigning features to phonemes in such a way that phonemes which behave similarly share common features. If both Mid tones and Lo tones cause Hi tones to be downstepped, for instance, this shared behavior should be reflected in their phonological representations.

Secondly, a model for tone needs to account (in an insightful manner) for the different types of tonal alternations found in natural language. These involve phenomena such as underlyingly toneless morphemes, "floating tones," all manner of assimilations and dissimilations, and register phenomena such as downstep and upstep. One of the most troublesome problems to overcome in trying to give a formal account of register phenomena is to explain the cumulative nature of downstep. In a sequence of downstepped Hi's, for example, each Hi is successively lower than its predecessor. It is therefore difficult for a model that permits only binary (or unary) valued features in the phonology component to be able to account for this.

Thirdly, a model for tone needs to be able to adequately characterize the different types of contour tones found in natural language. Yip (1989) describes contour tones as being of two types: those that function primarily as phonological units, and those that function primarily as phonological sequences of two or more level tones. Although contours of the first variety do function primarily as units, the beginning and end points of these contours often share certain characteristics with level tones, and a model for tone needs to be able to capture this.

Finally, a model for tone needs to be able to exclude from formal descriptions phenomena that never occur in natural language. Not only does Register Tier Theory (RTT) predict the existence of languages that exhibit certain tonal phenomena, but it also makes a number of predictions about what cannot exist. It predicts, for example, that no language will have more than six contrastive tone levels, that no language will have more than three falling (or rising) contours, and that no language will have more than three possibilities for feature assimilation: assimilation of register, assimilation of tone, and complete assimilation (i.e., assimilation of both register and tone).

An important tenet of RTT is that the levels of certain discrete tones are phonetically equivalent to the levels of certain other discrete tones that have been downstepped or upstepped. A downstepped Hi, for instance, is claimed to be phonetically equivalent to one of two possible Mid tones. By formally equating two levels like this, RTT can handle register phenomena such as downstep and upstep in the phonological component, together with other phenomena of comparable phonological status. This issue is controversial, and the present treatment provides a direct challenge to a number of other proposals (see §8.2) that account for downstep with phonetic implementation rules. These include Pierrehumbert (1980), Poser (1984), Beckman and Pierrehumbert (1986), and Pierrehumbert and Beckman (1988).

RTT grew out of attempts to account for the phenomena described above. Some of these attempts appear as book and journal articles, the succession of which reflects the development of the model. The present work adopts and continues to develop the model for representing tone advanced in Inkelas (1987, 1989), Inkelas and Leben (1991), Inkelas et al. (1987), Leben et al. (1989), and Snider (1988, 1990a, 1998). (Although the proposals of Inkelas et al. and of Snider were initially developed independently of each other, they are essentially the same.) Since each of these articles grapples with specific issues, it is difficult for the reader to "piece together" the model in a manner that permits him to apply it to his own data and problems. The present work, therefore, is a first attempt to provide a comprehensive overview of RTT. Chapter 1 introduces the uninitiated reader to the theory of Autosegmental Phonology. Those who already have a good understanding of this theory may wish to skip this chapter and go on to chapter 2. Chapters 2 and 3 form the heart of the work and together lay out the theory and its explanatory potential. Following this relatively abstract treatment of the theory, chapters 4 through 7 present case studies of diverse types of register phenomena. Finally, chapter 8 provides a critique of a number of alternative proposals that have appeared in the literature.

In order to reach as broad a readership as possible, the case studies have been prepared assuming a rule-based approach to generative phonology. Those readers who prefer Optimality Theory (OT) will find that the geometry and features of tone advanced in RTT also lend themselves quite nicely to insightful analyses in OT.

The model will undoubtedly continue to undergo development. If this stage of its development, however, proves to be even half as useful to the reader as it has been to the author, the effort expended by both parties in transferring this knowledge will be well-justified.

Over the years, many people have had positive input into the present work, and I wish to acknowledge their help. Harry van der Hulst was my co-promotor when I was a doctoral student at the University of Leiden. He believed in what I was doing and more than anyone else, helped shape at an early stage the ideas presented here. At about the same time, Nick Clements played a significant role in encouraging me and in helping me strengthen my arguments. Since that time, many people have made written comments on parts or all of the present volume, and I thank them for their constructive criticism. These include, in alphabetical order, Sean Allison, Erik Anonby, Steven Bird, Mike Cahill, Leslie Davis, Phil Davison, Robert Hedinger, Larry Hyman, Connie Kutsch Lojenga, David Morgan, Ngessimo Mutaka, Vaughn Ohlman, Larry Roetteger, Pat Rosendall, and Aaron Shryock. I owe a great debt to my colleague, Jim Roberts; more than anyone else, Jim has been my "sounding board" and has argued with me until I made sense. I have also profited from discussions with Rod Casali, Myles Leitch, and David Odden. Finally, Don Burquest, in his capacity as editor, made many suggestions that helped make this work more understandable to beginning linguists. In spite of all the help I have received, there undoubtedly remain mistakes and problems of which I am unaware, and I assume full responsibility for these. On the nonacademic side of things, I wish to thank my wife, Ruth, and sons, Lane, Marty, and Jeff, for "humouring" me to the end.

1
Autosegmental Phonology

1.1 Introduction

Register Tier Theory is an application of autosegmental phonology to tonal phenomena,[1] and so it will perhaps be helpful to begin with an overview of autosegmental phonology. As its name (autonomous segments) implies, autosegmental phonology assumes that there is a certain independence of features and segments. Traditionally, linguistic theory has viewed speech more or less as a horizontal stream that is chopped up into a linear sequence of units, or segments. Early generative phonology contributed to this the notion that each segment should be regarded as an unordered bundle of binary-valued distinctive features. In this framework the Chumburung[2] word *kánɔ́* 'mouth' has a phonological representation something like (1).

---

[1]Although it was investigations of tonal phenomena that led to the initial development of autosegmental phonology (e.g., Leben 1971, 1973 and Goldsmith 1976), its later development grew out of attempts to analyze nontonal phenomena. Unfortunately, these later developments did not find immediate application to tone. RTT, then, developed in response to this lacuna.

[2]Chumburung is a Kwa language spoken in Ghana. All Chumburung data in this book are taken from my personal field notes.

1

(1)   /k/   /a/   /n/   /ɔ/

         + Cons.   + Syllabic   + Cons.   + Syllabic

         − Nasal   − Nasal   + Nasal   − Nasal

         − Labial   − Labial   − Labial   + Labial

         − Coronal   − Coronal   + Coronal   − Coronal

            etc.   + High Tone   etc.   + High Tone

                            etc.   etc.

Missing from this is the (formal) recognition that between adjacent elements (segments, moras, and syllables) there is often a certain degree of continuity to the values assigned to individual features. Notice that in (1) both syllabic segments have a positive value for [High Tone]. Autosegmental phonology is able to capture these types of generalizations by viewing the speech stream as also being sliced into horizontal layers in such a way that features which behave as independent units are not represented as linear sequences of identical features. Instead, they occupy independent tiers and are *associated*, or *linked* to elements on other tiers by *association lines*. Early autosegmental work represented a word like *kánɔ́* as in (2).[3]

(2)

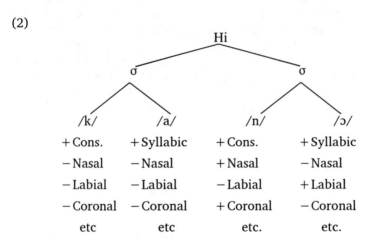

---

[3]Following Hyman (1992), I assume that the mora (μ) is the TBU. In earlier autosegmental representations, however, the syllable (σ) was considered to be the TBU.

In (2) the Hi tone occupies the tonal tier and is associated to the two syllables of the word. Although the Hi is phonetically realized on two syllables, in other respects it acts as a unit. When lowering due to downstep[4] occurs, for example, all the syllables associated to the Hi are affected. By representing tone autosegmentally then, both the unitary and the plural natures of the Hi tone are respected.

Although the purpose of this overview is to introduce the uninitiated reader to the basics of autosegmental theory (as opposed to convincing the reader of its validity), it will be helpful to go over some of the advantages of representing tone autosegmentally.[5]

1.2 Advantages of autosegmental representations

We first consider the matter of contour tones. There are problems if we consider the tonal properties associated with any given vowel to be an inherent part of the vocalic phoneme itself, and also hold to the view that phonemes are *unordered* bundles of binary-valued distinctive features. In an early application of generative phonology to tone problems, Wang (1967) proposed the features [Rising] and [Falling] to account for tonal contours. While in some parts of the world (e.g., Asia) contour tones are more or less indivisible, in other parts of the world (e.g., Africa) they are clearly a concatenation of two or more level tones, a fact which cannot be accounted for using features like [Rising] and [Falling]. In order to remedy this situation, Woo (1969) proposed that contour tones are actually sequences of level tones which are realized over two or more adjacent sonorants. While this works fine for contours that involve long vowels or sequences of vowels and sonorant consonants, it predicts that contour tones are never realized on short vowels, a restriction that has since proven not to be valid. Work by Leben (1971, 1973) demonstrates that contours of the level-tone-sequence variety also occur on short vowels. If tone is part of the feature specification of the vocalic phoneme, and if phonemes are unordered bundles of distinctive features, there is no way to represent a short vowel with, say, a Hi-Lo contour tone in a manner that

---

[4]As discussed in chapter 3, downstep is the assimilation of a Hi or Mid tone to the lower register of an adjacent (usually preceding) Lo tone. When the Lo tone is associated, or nonfloating, as in (5), the downstep is called *automatic downstep*, or sometimes *downdrift*. When th Lo tone is unassociated, or floating, as in (6), it is called *nonautomatic downstep*, or simply *downstep*.

[5]For a more "in depth" review of the motivation for, and the principles that govern autosegmental phonology, the interested reader is referred to Goldsmith (1990) and Kenstowicz (1994).

respects the integrity of the Hi and Lo tones involved. This argues against tone being considered an inherent part of segmental representation.

In autosegmental theory, a contour tone is represented as two tones "mapped" onto a single TBU (tone-bearing unit). This is demonstrated in (3). Compare (3) with (2), which is the converse, i.e., a single tone mapped onto two TBUs.

(3)   a. Rising Tone   b. Falling Tone

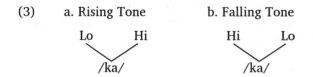

(3a) represents a concatenation of the level tones Lo and Hi on a single TBU (realized as a rising tone), and (3b) represents a concatenation of the level tones Hi and Lo on a single TBU (realized as a falling tone). By representing tone autosegmentally, the problems that contour tones posed for preautosegmental generative phonology are overcome.

Crosslinguistically, it has been discovered that the underlying tonal melodies (i.e., the underlying sequences of tones) associated with morphemes in any given language are relatively few in number. A second case for representing tone autosegmentally can therefore be made from the restrictions languages place on the combinations of tones found in morphemes. For any given language, the combinations of tones is not completely arbitrary. In monomorphemic words in Mende, for example (data from Leben 1978), monosyllabic forms with short vowels may have any one of the following five contrastive tonal melodies: Hi, Lo, Falling, Rising, or Rising-Falling. A classical phonemic analysis of this would yield five "tonemes" with, theoretically, 125 possible combinations of tonemes on trisyllabic morphemes. The language does not take advantage of all these possibilities, however. In fact, for each class of morphemes (monosyllabic, disyllabic, etc.), one finds only five different melodies, or "melodemes" employed, and these five correspond directly to the five found on monosyllabic morphemes.

(4)		One-Syllable		Two-Syllable		Three-Syllable	
Hi		kɔ́	'war'	pélé	'house'	háwámá	'waistline'
Lo		kpà	'debt'	bèlè	'trousers'	kpàkàlì	'tripod chair'
Hi Lo		mbû	'owl'	ngílà	'dog'	félàmà	'junction'
Lo Hi		mbǎ	'rice'	fàndé	'cotton'	ndàvúlá	'sling'
Lo Hi Lo		mbã̌	'companion'	nyã̂hâ	'woman'	nìkílì	'groundnut'

For any given morpheme in Mende then, the native speaker needs to associate with it only one of five tonal melodies. Using autosegmental theory, one can analyze Mende as a two-level system with five tonal melodies that associate to TBUs in an insightful manner, as opposed to a five-toneme system with tonemes that associate to TBUs in an unexplainable manner.

A third case for representing tone autosegmentally can be made from the stability of tonal melodies. In tone languages, when a TBU is lost for whatever reason (e.g., vowel elision, apocope), its tone normally remains in one form or another. Often it shifts its location and surfaces on another TBU, either altogether displacing the original tone of the second TBU, or joining with it to form a contour if the two tones are different. At other times, its effect is realized on adjacent tones in the form of lowering due to downstep. We see examples of each of these phenomena in these next Ghotuo examples, taken from Elugbe (1986).

(5)   ɔ́ gbé ɔ̀sɛ̄   →   [ɔ́ gbɔ̂ˈsɛ̄]   'he killed a cricket'

In (5), despite the loss of the vowel e, the Hi of the underlying melody remains and forms a contour with the following Lo. The presence of the Lo also causes the following Mid to be downstepped, or lowered relative to the first Mid tone. Downstep is indicated here and elsewhere by the down arrow. Example (6) is an acceptable variant of (5) in certain Ghotuo dialects.

(6)   ɔ́ gbé ɔ̀sɛ̄   →   [ɔ́ gbɔ́ˈsɛ̄]   'he killed a cricket'

In (6) the Hi also remains, despite the loss of the e, but in this case, it entirely displaces the underlying Lo from the vowel ɔ. Although the Lo itself does not appear in the surface form of (6), its presence is nevertheless confirmed by the downstepping of the following Mid.

The stability of the Hi tone in (5) and (6) is captured in autosegmental theory by its continued residence on the tonal tier. The fact that it is phonetically realized in different places in different environments (e.g., on the vowel e in one environment, and on the vowel ɔ in another environment) is captured in autosegmental theory by the different segments to which it is associated. This is shown in the derivation of (5) in (7). At this point, no attempt is made to account for downstep.

(7)   a. Underlying Form   b. Vowel Deletion

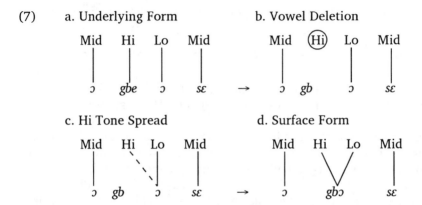

     c. Hi Tone Spread   d. Surface Form

In (7b), despite the loss of its TBU, the Hi tone remains as a floating tone (indicated by its being circled). In (7c), the floating Hi spreads (indicated by the dotted association line) to the TBU to its right where, together with the following Lo, it forms a falling contour.

These facts, taken together, argue strongly for representing tone on a tier separate from segmental material.

1.3 Principles of autosegmental phonology

So far, we have seen some of the advantages in representing tone on a separate tier, but we have not yet discussed how the tonal and segmental tiers relate to one another. Languages exercise a number of options with regard to this relationship. In the case of specific morphemes, a morpheme can logically consist of:

     a. a segmental "melody" and a tonal melody (the normal case),
     b. a tonal melody without a segmental melody (i.e., a floating tone), or
     c. a segmental melody without a tonal melody (i.e., a toneless
        morpheme).

Each of these options occurs in natural languages, and it is not uncommon to find all three occurring in one language.

If we consider the Mende data in (4) it is clear that regardless of how many syllables a morpheme has, the tonal melody associated with it is mapped onto it in a principled manner. How this is done in any given language, however, is not completely arbitrary since cross-linguistically, it can be seen that the conventions that govern the association of tones to TBUs are nearly universal. The association conventions may be stated as follows:

(8)   Association Conventions:
        For any given morpheme, map the individual tones of its tonal melody onto its tone-bearing units,

        (a) from left to right
        (b) in a one-to-one relation.

   A second tenet of autosegmental theory is the WELL-FORMEDNESS CONDI-TION, which Pulleyblank (1986:11) states as follows:

(9)   Well-formedness Condition:
        Association lines do not cross.

   When there are more TBUs than tones, the final tone often associates to the left-over TBUs, and when there are fewer TBUs than tones, the left-over tones often associate to the final TBU. How any given language handles situations in which there is not a one-to-one correlation, however, is considered to be language-specific, and whatever strategies the language employs to correct any mismatches (e.g., final tone association, vowel lengthening, etc.) are often not carried out until later in a derivation. The following examples show how application of the association conventions yield the correct tonal forms for the Mende examples in (4).

(10)   Three tones, three TBUs

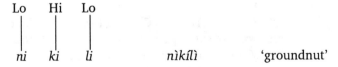

                 nìkílì   'groundnut'

   In (10), the melody associated with the morpheme is Lo Hi Lo, and the tones are associated from left to right and one-to-one.

(11)   Two tones, three TBUs

ndàvúlá   'sling'

In (11), the tonal melody associated with the morpheme is Lo Hi. The tones are again associated to the TBUs from left to right and one-to-one. Since there are more TBUs than tones, the final tone spreads to the remaining TBU.

(12)   Three tones, two TBUs

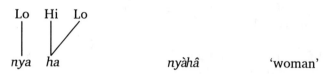

nyàhâ   'woman'

In (12), the tonal melody associated with the morpheme is Lo Hi Lo, the same as that in (10). The tones are again associated from left to right and one-to-one, but in this case there is one tone left over. In some languages, this tone would just remain floating, or in certain cases be deleted. In Mende, however, the remaining tone associates to the final TBU to form a high-low falling contour.

Another principle that appears to be well-motivated in autosegmental phonology is called the OBLIGATORY CONTOUR PRINCIPLE, or OCP. This is stated as follows:

(13)   Obligatory Contour Principle:
        Adjacent identical features are prohibited on the same tier.

Work by Odden (1986, 1988a) and McCarthy (1986) on whether or not the OCP is a universal constraint suggests that instead of being a single principle as such, the OCP is a cover term for a set of principles that "conspire" to produce a (nearly) universal OCP effect.[6] Although it is generally agreed that the OCP is a valid principle, exactly *when* it applies remains the subject of controversy. The present work adopts a fairly strict version of the OCP and assumes that morphemes in their underlying forms do not have identical tones adjacent to one another. Monomorphemic forms, like

---

[6]The analysis in chapter 6 of upstep in Acatlán Mixtec is one example of where the OCP is assumed *not* to apply.

the Mende word *bèlè* 'trousers' in (14), therefore, do not have a sequence of two Lo tones, but rather have one Lo tone that is spread over two TBUs.

(14)   Monomorphemic form

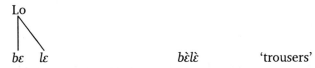

bɛ lɛ   *bèlè*   'trousers'

The present work also assumes that following word formation processes, a process called MERGER applies in many languages. Merger is the coalescence of identical adjacent features and is one of the most common repair strategies languages employ in order to satisfy OCP constraints. When Merger applies, it applies *whenever* it can (i.e., as soon as its structural description is met). Forms like the Bamileke-Dschang word *è-fɔ* 'chief', which has two Lo tones in its underlying form because it is composed of two morphemes, are therefore subject to Merger.

(15)   Bimorphemic form

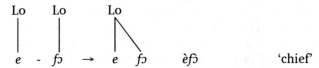

e - fɔ   →   e   fɔ   *èfɔ*   'chief'

In (15), the two underlying Lo tones are coalesced by Merger. We discuss the role of the OCP in tone phenomena in more depth in chapter 2.

We turn now to some of the notation conventions that exist with regard to autosegmental representations. When discussing autosegmental representations, it is helpful to know the terms ARGUMENT AND TARGET. An argument is the element that undergoes a rule. If we say, for example, that a Hi tone spreads or is deleted, the Hi tone is the argument. A target can be described as the element which is at the opposite end of the (actual or proposed) association line from the argument. In the case of the Hi tone spreading rules we have discussed, the targets have been TBUs. Although most of the conventions that are used to formalize graphic representations have already been presented informally, they are summarized in (16).[7]

---

[7](16) is an adaptation of Katamba's (1989:197) presentation of autosegmental notation.

(16)   Notation conventions of graphic representations:

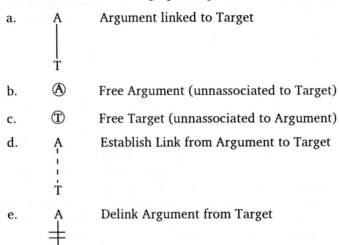

a.   A   Argument linked to Target
      |
      |
      T

b.   Ⓐ   Free Argument (unnassociated to Target)

c.   Ⓣ   Free Target (unnassociated to Argument)

d.   A   Establish Link from Argument to Target
      ¦
      ¦
      ¦
      T

e.   A   Delink Argument from Target
      ‡
      |
      T

It is also helpful to understand the various options that exist with regard to the application of autosegmental rules. While it might at first seem that the number of options associated with autosegmental rules is great, this is not so; the theory is actually highly constrained. In their work *Grounded Phonology*, Archangeli and Pulleyblank (1994:286–93) identify four parameters that govern the application of autosegmental rules: FUNCTION, TYPE, DIRECTION, and ITERATION. Although we will not be adopting all of Archangeli and Pulleyblank's terminology, an understanding of the parameters they identify will prove useful. We discuss each parameter in turn.

Function deals with whether a PATH or F-ELEMENT (feature-element) is inserted or deleted. In simple terms, paths are association lines, and F-elements are the features and structural elements that the association lines join. (The only F-elements that have been introduced so far are tones and TBUs.) Consider the rule of Ghotuo Hi Tone Spread that was assumed in (7c). Graphically, this rule can be depicted as in (17).

(17)   Graphic representation of Ghotuo Hi Tone Spread (HTS)

Hi   Lo

μ

In (17), a floating Hi tone spreads rightwards to the first TBU. For this rule, the Function is INSERT, and in this case the inserted material is a PATH, or association line. The other option for the Function parameter is for something to be deleted. In many languages, when HTS occurs, a following Lo tone is delinked (represented by two short parallel lines that cross the association line in question). HTS and Lo Tone Delink are rules in Chumburung.

(18)   Chumburung HTS and Lo Tone Delink

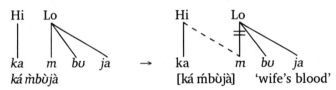

According to Archangeli and Pulleyblank, this type of delinking would involve a second rule in which the Function parameter is set for DELETE; in this case, the deletion would involve the path between the Lo tone and the TBU *m*.

Type deals with whether a rule inserts or deletes a path or an F-element. We have already discussed insertion and deletion of paths. Insertion and deletion of F-elements includes things like the assignment of a default Lo tone to a toneless morpheme at the end of the phonological derivation (more on this later). It also includes things like the deletion of floating tones in certain contexts.

(19)   a. Default Lo insertion   b. Lo deletion

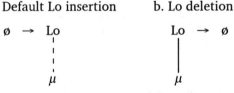

Direction deals with the direction a particular rule applies in. Spreading, for instance, can occur either left to right or right to left.

(20)   a. HTS: left to right   b. HTS: right to left

Iterativity deals with whether or not a given rule's application is iterative or noniterative. In the case of a HTS rule, a noniterative application would mean that the Hi tone would spread only to the next TBU. On the other hand, an iterative application would mean that the Hi tone would spread to as many TBUs as possible.

(21)   a. HTS: iterative   b. HTS: noniterative

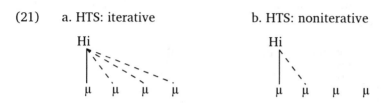

Archangeli and Pulleyblank's four parameters are summarized in (22).

(22)   Parameters of autosegmental rules

Function:	insert	delete
Type:	path	F-element
Direction:	left to right	right to left
Iteration:	iterative	noniterative

In autosegmental phonology, rules can be formalized using either of two notations: (a) parametric formulations (along the lines suggested by Archangeli and Pulleyblank), or (b) graphic representations. Graphic representations are the older (with respect to the development of the theory) type of formalism and are what we are using in the present work. Although there are certain problems inherent in this type of formalism,[8] graphic representations are easier to interpret than parametric formulations and so have greater expository value.

1.4 Excursus on lexical phonology

Throughout the case studies that appear in later chapters, a crucial distinction is sometimes made between lexical and postlexical rules. A brief excursus on LEXICAL PHONOLOGY is therefore in order.

---

[8]For an enlightening discussion on this topic, the interested reader is referred to chapter 4 of Archangeli and Pulleyblank (1994).

Lexical phonology is actually a synthesis of two theories, a theory of phonology and a theory of morphological word-formation rules. In the course of its development, some of the more influential works to emerge included Kiparsky (1982a), an abridged version of which appeared as Kiparsky (1982b), Kiparsky (1985), and Mohanan's (1982) doctoral dissertation, published as Mohanan (1986). Example (23) illustrates how the model is organized.

(23)   Lexical phonology model

Lexical Component

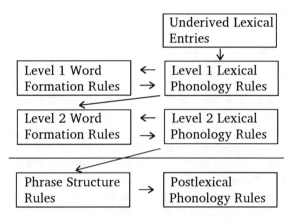

Postlexical Component

Rules fall into two broad classes, lexical and postlexical. Whereas lexical rules apply to the results of word formation processes, postlexical or phrasal rules apply to the results of phrase formation. The two classes are further distinguished as follows:

Lexical Rules	Postlexical Rules
1. There may be lexical exceptions.	Apply across the board without exception.
2. Can lack phonetic motivation.	Never lack phonetic motivation.

3.	Preserve structure; i.e., the output of a rule is a contrastive (phonemic) element.	Are not necessarily structure preserving.
4.	Native speakers are aware of the rules' applications.	Rules operate below the level of native awareness.
5.	May refer to the internal structure of a word.	May never refer to the internal structure of a word.
6.	May never refer to the internal structure of a phrase (e.g., word boundaries, end of phrase, etc.).	May refer to the internal structure of a phrase.
7.	Are subject to cyclicity.	Are not cyclic. They only apply once.
8.	Apply before postlexical rules.	Apply after lexical rules.

Although, as mentioned above, the present work sometimes distinguishes between lexical and postlexical rules, it does not refer crucially to differences between the different levels or strata within the lexical component. The reader should be aware, however, that in any one language, morphological processes typically divide into two classes, based on how the phonology deals with the results of the morphological processes. This means that some phonological rules may apply to the output of some morphological processes but not to others. Within the model, these different classes of morphological processes correspond to the different levels, or strata, in the lexical component. Normally, there are not more than two levels in the lexical component, although some linguists have posited three (or more) for English.

1.5 Hierarchical structure

So far, we have looked only at tone. Autosegmental phonology also gives a very satisfactory account of nontonal phenomena. Vowel harmony systems based on features like [Advanced Tongue Root, (ATR)], [Round], and [Nasal] for instance, have proven very amenable to autosegmental analysis. In autosegmental phonology, assimilation processes are accounted for by spreading rules. Example (24) demonstrates the leftwards spreading of the feature [Advanced Tongue Root] from a noun to a possessive pronoun in Chumburung.

(24)   Leftward spreading of the feature [Advanced Tongue Root]

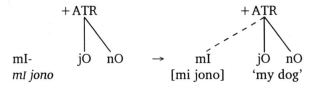

mI-   jO nO   →   mI   jO nO   'my dog'
mI jono   [mi jono]

With the proliferation of tiers that comes as a result of many features occupying separate tiers, there arises the question of how all these tiers relate to one another. One possible way, suggested (and then rejected) by
Clements (1985), is for all the feature tiers to associate to one core, or
"skeletal" tier, in a three-dimensional "pinwheel" structure like (25).[9]

(25)   Nonhierarchical organization of autosegmental tiers

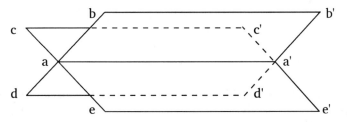

aa' = CV tier, *bb'* = tonal tier, *cc'* = ATR tier, *dd'* = voiced tier,
ee' = nasal tier

According to Clements, representations like (25) can be thought of as an
open "book" in which the spine (*aa'*) corresponds to the skeleton CV (consonant, vowel) tier, and the outer edges of the pages (*bb'*, *cc'*, etc.) correspond to the other tiers. Structures like this allow one to represent
"processes that affect features on one tier while not affecting features on
the others" (1985:228). In this way then, processes like spreading that
would involve the tonal and skeletal tiers do not interfere with other
processes that would involve, say, the ATR and skeletal tiers. Structures
like (25), however, treat all features as equal, and in so doing fail to recognize the fact that some features group with others into sets which behave
as units. For example, in many languages, a nasal consonant is realized as
m before *p*, *n* before *t*, and *ŋ* before *k*, etc. If we assume that each place feature (i.e., point of articulation) occupies its own tier, and assume the

---

[9]I wish to thank Cambridge University Press for permission to include an adaptation of di-
agrams (2) and (3) from pages 227 and 229, respectively, of Clements (1985) as (25) and (29).

structure of (25), we have representations like (26). These Chumburung examples demonstrate spreading of the place feature of the first consonant of the root onto the syllabic nasal consonant of the noun class prefix. Because syllabic nasals in Chumburung always precede consonants, and they always assimilate to the place features of those consonants, there is no reason to assume that they have any underlying specification for place.

(26)   a. Nonhierarchical representation of feature [Labial] in Chumburung

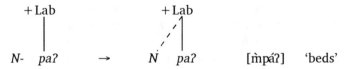

N- pa?   →   N pa?   [m̀pá?]   'beds'

b. Nonhierarchical representation of feature [Back] in Chumburung

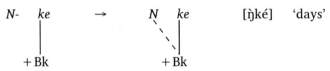

N- ke   →   N ke   [ŋ̀ké]   'days'

The representations in (26) have multiple rules for spreading the place features; that is, one rule for each place feature, since each feature occupies its own tier. This is less than ideal, however, as will be shown. Nasal consonants not only assimilate to the place of articulation of *ps* and *ks* in Chumburung, but they also assimilate to the place of doubly articulated consonants like *kp*, with the result that preceding nasal consonants are realized as *ŋm*.

(27)   Nasal assimilation to *kp*

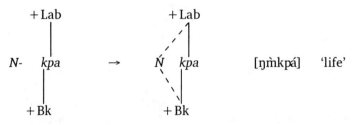

N- kpa   →   Ń kpa   [ŋm̀kpá]   'life'

Requiring two rules to represent the assimilation of the nasal consonant to the place of articulation of a following *kp* is not very satisfactory because this assimilation is essentially a single process. One step towards overcoming this problem would be to assume that all place features occupy a single (place) tier, instead of each occupying its own separate tier. One could then have a single rule that would spread the place feature of the consonant, whatever it is, to the preceding nasal consonant. While this would work for the examples in (26), it would not work for the example in (27), which involves a doubly articulated consonant. This is demonstrated in (28).

(28)   Place features on same tier (violates Well-formedness Condition)

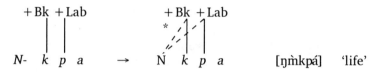

                 [ŋm̀kpá] 'life'

There are two serious problems with (28). First, placing the features [Back] and [Labial] on the same autosegmental tier demands that there exist a linear ordering between them, either [Back, Labial], or [Labial, Back]. But in the case of doubly articulated consonants, for all practical purposes both features are articulated simultaneously.[10] The second problem is that the crossing of association lines that would be involved in order for the nasal consonant to be associated to both features would violate the Well-formedness Condition of (9).

Rather than representing several assimilation processes (one for each feature) for what is obviously one process, Clements proposes that classes of features, like place features, associate to class tiers, and that these class tiers themselves associate to other (greater) class tiers in a hierarchical structure like (29).

---

[10]Recent work on labial-velar stops shows that the durations of the two articulations overlap for the most part, but "most frequently the velar closure precedes the labial one, while the labial release is subsequent to the velar one" (Connell 1994:274). Since the misalignment of the two articulations is only slight, it is not yet clear what (if any) implications exist for feature geometry.

(29)   Hierarchical Organization of Class Tiers

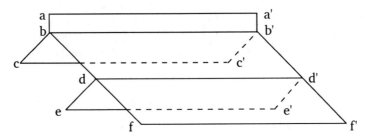

aa' = CV tier, *bb'* = root tier, *cc'* = laryngeal tier, *dd'* = supralaryngeal sier, *ee'* = manner tier, *ff* = place pier

In (29), the tiers *bb'* through *ff* represent class tiers. Not shown here are the feature tiers that associate to their respective class tiers in the same manner as the feature tiers of (25) associate to the CV tier.

We now apply a structure like (29) to the problem, raised earlier, concerning the assimilation of nasal consonants to the point of articulation of following consonants. Throughout the remainder of this work, representations like (30) can be thought of as "end views" of three-dimensional structures like (29).

(30)   Consonant place spreading in Chumburung

a.

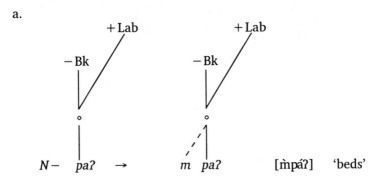

b.

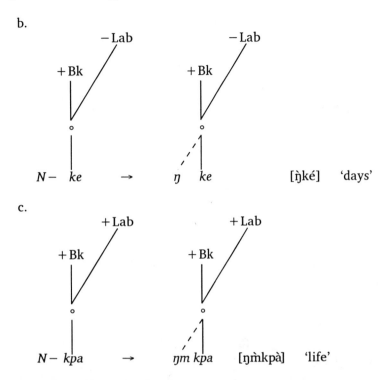

$N-$ *ke*   →   ŋ *ke*   [ŋ̀ké]   'days'

c.

ŋm *kpa*   [ŋ̀mkpà]   'life'

$N-$ *kpa*   →

In (30), regardless of the specification for place, there is only one process involved (viz., spreading from the place node). The model in (31), taken from Kenstowicz (1994:146), is based on proposals by Halle (1992) and serves to illustrate how some linguists believe the feature tree for segmental (i.e., nontonal) material is organized.[11, 12]

[11]For more in-depth presentations of autosegmental phonology, the interested reader is referred to Goldsmith (1990), Katamba (1989), and Kenstowicz (1994).

[12]I wish to thank Blackwell Publishers for permission to include diagram (3) on page 146 from chapter 4 of Kenstowicz (1994) as example (31).

(31)   Feature geometry model

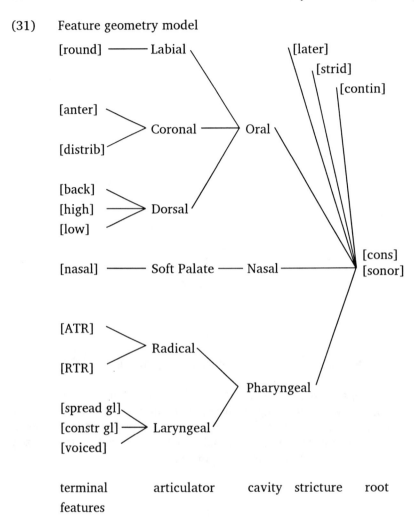

          terminal   articulator   cavity   stricture   root
          features

How many tiers exist, what tiers exist, and how the tiers are organized continue to be questions that drive ongoing research in autosegmental theory. The remainder of the present work focuses on that part of this investigation which pertains to tone.

2
Register Tier Theory

Chapter 1 gave a brief overview of autosegmental theory, and demonstrated some of the advantages of representing tone autosegmentally. Apart from §1.4, the geometry employed was restricted to two tiers: a segmental tier and a tonal tier. The segmental tier consisted of a string of consonant and vowel phonemes that constituted the *segmental* melodies of morphemes, and the tonal tier consisted of a string of tone phonemes that constituted the *tonal* melodies of morphemes. In §1.4 we saw that viewing the segmental tier as a tier in and of itself was really an oversimplification. Rather than being a single tier as such, it is instead a composition of many tiers that are arranged in a hierarchical geometric structure. In a similar way, viewing the tonal tier as a tier in and of itself is also an oversimplification. This chapter provides an overview of the composition of what up until now has been called the tonal tier.

2.1 Tone and register

In order to better understand the phonological geometry and features that are needed to represent natural tone systems, we begin with an analogy between tone and music. Linguistic tones can be likened to the musical notes that make up a simple melody. While it is possible to play a simple melody on a musical instrument in, say, the key of A, it is also possible to play that same melody in a higher or lower key. In other words, the key, or register can be shifted up or down. Tone languages also employ the concept of register. For example, in many African tone languages, downstep occurs with the result that any Hi tone that follows the point of downstep is lower in pitch than any Hi tone that precedes the point of downstep. Similarly, any Lo that follows the point of downstep is lower in pitch than any Lo that precedes the point of downstep. In the surface (phonetic) representations throughout the remainder of this work, the horizontal dotted lines represent the tonal registers, and the solid lines represent the pitch of each TBU relative to the current register; i.e., the (idealized) pitch traces of the utterances.

(32)   Downstep in Chumburung

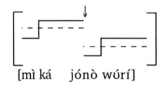

[mì ká   jónò wúrí]   'his wife's dog's skin'

In this Chumburung example, we can think of the Lo Hi Hi sequence that precedes the point of downstep as a two-note melody, or tune written in, say, the key of A, represented by the leftmost dotted line. The Lo Hi Hi sequence that follows the point of downstep could then be considered to be the same melody transposed into the key of A-flat, represented by the rightmost dotted line. There is one further observation to make from (32). Notice that the first Lo tone of the utterance and the final two Hi tones are realized at the same pitch. While this situation does not hold for all downstepping languages, it does hold for downstep in Chumburung. Continuing our analogy to music, this would be analogous to a certain musical note being called, say, C-sharp in the key of A, but D-flat in the key of A-flat on the even-tempered scale of modern-day pianos. We discuss this further below.

At this point the analogy between linguistic melodies and music melodies begins to break down. While simple music melodies may employ many different notes in any given key, I will demonstrate that linguistic melodies never employ more than two tones on any given register. And while simple music melodies are usually confined to single keys, tonal melodies (especially of phonological phrases) are not normally confined to single registers.

2.2 Geometry of tone

Register Tier Theory[13] recognizes the following autosegmental features and tiers: the register features h and l on a REGISTER TIER, the tonal features H and L on a TONAL TIER, a TONAL ROOT NODE (TRN) TIER, and a TONE-BEARING UNIT TIER. These tiers are geometrically arranged according to the configuration in (33).

(33)   Geometry of tone

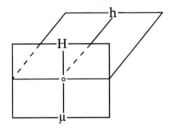

Register tier

Tonal tier

Tonal root node tier

Tonal-bearing unit tier

Features on the Register tier and the Tonal tier are linked to structural nodes on the TRN tier. Geometrically, these tiers form separate planes with respect to the TRN tier. Nodes on the TRN tier are, in turn, linked to moras (μ) on the TBU tier.

The features (discussed in §2.3) and geometry of (33) logically allow one to fully specify up to four level tone phonemes: Hi, Mid$_2$, Mid$_1$, and Lo. Phonological representations for each phoneme[14] appear in (34), and phonetic representations appear in (35).

---

[13]This model is very much in the spirit of Clements (1983) and Hyman (1985, 1986), and it owes a great deal of its inspiration to them. For comparisons with and critiques of these and other proposals for the representation of tone (including Pulleyblank 1986), the interested reader is referred to Inkelas et al. (1987), Inkelas and Leben (1991), and Snider (1988, 1990a).

[14]As stated, these representations are *fully* specified; underspecification theory is dealt with in §2.4.

(34)   a.   b.   c.   d.

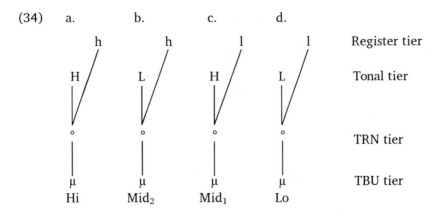

(35)   Phonetic representation of four level tone phonemes

$\overline{\text{H}\uparrow}$

- - - - - - $\overline{\text{H}\uparrow}$

            L↓   - - - - - -

                                L↓

    Hi   Mid₂   Mid₁   Lo

The lower case *hs* and *ls* on the Register tier in (34), respectively denote higher and lower registers, and these are represented in (35) by the higher and lower dotted lines. Similarly, the upper case *Hs* and *Ls* on the Tonal tier in (34), respectively denote high and low pitch relative to the current register, and these are represented in (35) by the solid lines above and below the dotted register lines.

2.3 Features of tone

So far in this chapter, the phonological features of the model have not yet been defined, although they have been used in order to demonstrate the geometry. One of the most difficult problems to overcome in arriving at a feature system for tone phonemes is the fact that the acoustic and articulatory properties of tone are relative in nature. A surface Hi tone, for example, has a higher fundamental frequency and is articulated with greater vocal cord tension than is a surface Lo tone in the same environment, say, Environment A. But in another environment, say Environment B, a surface Lo tone might be realized with the same acoustic and articulatory properties as the surface Hi tone of Environment A. By way of contrast, segments have acoustic and articulatory properties that fall within reasonably well-defined ranges. For any given speaker, a surface *e* in Environment A would never be realized with the acoustic and articulatory properties of a surface *i* in Environment B. For this reason, the tonal features of RTT are defined relatively.

I define the register features *h* and *l* as, "Effect a register shift *h* = higher, and *l* = lower relative to the preceding register setting," and the tonal features *H* and *L* as, "Realize this TBU at *H* = high pitch, and *L* = low pitch relative to the current register." This is shown in (36).[15] As stated earlier, the dotted lines in the examples represent registers and the solid lines represent tones.

(36)   Register features and tonal features

$$
\begin{array}{ccc}
 & & \overline{\text{H}}\uparrow \\
\overline{\text{H}}\uparrow & h \; \nearrow \; \text{-- -- -- -- --} & \\
\text{-- -- -- -- --} & \diagdown & \overline{\text{H}}\uparrow \quad \text{L}\!\downarrow \\
\underline{\text{L}}\!\downarrow & l \; \searrow \; \text{-- -- -- -- --} & \\
 & & \underline{\text{L}}\!\downarrow \\
\end{array}
$$

The register feature associated to any given TBU specifies whether the register of that TBU is higher or lower than the preceding register. This raises the question of how to interpret the register feature of the first TBU in an utterance, since there is no preceding TBU. I assume that native speakers begin all utterances with a reference point in mind. For the initial TBU then, the register could be higher than or lower than this reference point. The tonal feature associated to any given TBU specifies whether the tone is high or low relative to the current register. Consider the following representations.

---

[15]This diagram was inspired by Jim Roberts.

(37)   Typical Hi-Lo sequence

     a. Structural representation   b. Phonetic representation

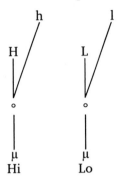 

      μ   μ   μ   μ
      Hi   Lo   Hi   Lo

    In (37), the first TBU is realized with a H tone on its register. Because the second TBU is associated to a register l that is not linked to the preceding TBU, the L of this TBU is realized on a lower register than that of the preceding TBU. (If the l *were* linked to the preceding TBU, the tones of both TBUs would be realized on the same register.) In interpreting the phonetic representations in (37) and elsewhere, upper case Hs and Ls, together with up and down arrows, represent the tones of the TBUs relative to their registers. By way of contrast, lower case ls and hs, together with slanted arrows, represent the changes in register (higher or lower) between TBUs.

    The next example represents a typical downstep situation in which the second Hi of a Hi-Lo-Hi sequence is downstepped relative to the first Hi.

(38)   Automatic downstepped Hi

   a. Input   b. *l*-Spread

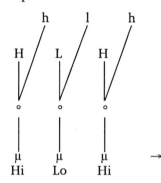

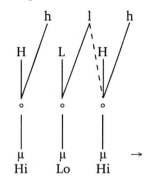

   c. Delink   d. Phonetic representation

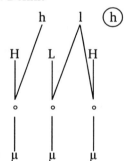

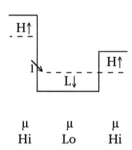

   The input to automatic downstep is shown in (38a). In (38b) the register feature *l* of the Lo tone spreads rightwards to the TRN of the following Hi tone, and in (38c) the register feature *h* of the following Hi tone is delinked and set floating (indicated by the circle). In the phonetic representation of (38d), the first two TBUs are interpreted in a manner identical to that of the first two TBUs in (37), i.e., there is a tonal difference *and* a register difference between the first and second TBUs. Since the third TBU is associated to the same register feature as the second TBU, the *H* of this TBU is realized on the same (lower) register as that of the *L* of the second TBU. This means that the second Hi tone is downstepped relative to the first Hi.
   Next consider the treatment of an automatic downstepped Hi that is followed by Lo. Rather than show all the steps of the derivation as in (38), in (39) we adopt some of the shorthand conventions of autosegmental phonology that were presented in chapter 1.

(39)   Automatic downstepped Hi followed by Lo

      a. Structural representation   b. Phonetic representation

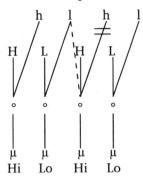

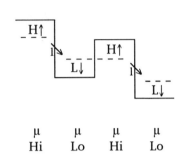

    μ   μ   μ   μ   μ   μ   μ   μ

   Hi Lo Hi Lo   Hi Lo Hi Lo

In (39), the same situation obtains for the first three TBUs as was the case in (38). The pitch of the fourth TBU requires some explanation. Since it is associated to a register *l*, it is interpreted as being realized on a register lower than that of the preceding TBU, provided the preceding TBU is not also linked to that same register *l*. In this case it is not. Even though both TBUs are linked to register *ls*, the TBUs are not linked to the *same* register feature, so the register automatically lowers at this point. Notice that Merger cannot coalesce the two *ls* because there is an intervening *h*. (Recall that tone melodies are relatively stable, and that even though tone features are occasionally delinked from their tone-bearing units, their existence continues on their respective autosegmental tiers.) Notice also that the height of the fourth TBU relative to that of the third TBU is the same as that of the second TBU relative to the first TBU. In both cases, the *L* tone that follows the *H* is on a lower register than the *H*.

2.4 Underspecification

In order to present the model as clearly as possible, the phonological representations up to this point have all been fully specified, i.e., every TBU has been specified for both register and tone, and every register and tone feature has been associated to a TBU. The present work assumes, however, that not all phonological information is fully specified in underlying forms.

The notion that underlying phonological representations are not fully specified receives impetus from at least two sources. The first is the intuitively satisfying assumption of early generative grammar that the rules of a language account for all predictable information, and the lexicon is the repository for all unpredictable information. But given that language has redundancy built in at virtually all levels, the notion that there is no redundancy in underlying forms has not gone unchallenged. Nevertheless, it is generally agreed that there is at least a certain amount of underspecification in underlying forms. The second, and stronger, source of impetus for the notion of underspecification comes from the observation that in many languages the application of spreading processes is often blocked in certain environments. This blockage is most easily accounted for by assuming that when spreading occurs, it takes place when the segments undergoing the spreading are unspecified for a certain feature, and that the spreading is blocked when these segments are specified for that feature. Underspecification is used to advantage in this manner in some of the case studies that appear in later chapters.[16]

The present work departs from previous proposals of RTT in assuming that register features are primary, and tonal features secondary; that is, tonal features are underspecified before register features. This departure makes for simpler analyses in the following way. Often the sole indicator of an underlying floating Lo tone is that it downsteps a following Hi.[17] If the tonal feature L were underlying, then the register feature l that causes the downstep would have to be assigned later by default, and still later the original L, which never did anything other than trigger the assignment of the l, would be deleted by STRAY ERASURE (see end of §2.5). The analysis is more straightforward if the register feature l that causes the downstep is simply present from the beginning.

One assumption made in the present work is that adjacent TRNs that meet the structural description of the same default feature assignment rule are assigned the *same* default feature. Motivation for this assumption comes, on the one hand, from languages like Acatlán Mixtec (see chapter 6), which are not subject to OCP merging constraints, yet appear to assign a single default Lo tone to adjacent toneless TBUs. On the other hand, Kenstowicz (1994) argues convincingly that adjacent TBUs are assigned unique default Lo tones in at least Shona and Venda. At this point in time, I leave the question open. Whether or not this assumption is correct is a moot point for most languages because if the default feature assignment rule assigned unique identical default features to adjacent TRNs, they

---

[16]For more in-depth treatments of underspecification, the interested reader is referred to Archangeli (1988), Goldsmith (1990), and Kenstowicz (1994).

[17]The notion of downstep (automatic and nonautomatic) was introduced in chapter 1 (footnote 4) and is discussed in more detail in chapter 3.

would later be merged anyway since most languages are subject to OCP merging constraints. We return to this point in chapter 6.

The underlying representation in (40) is typical of many surface "two-tone" systems. Following Snider (1990a), each TBU is assumed to be associated to a unique TRN in underlying forms.

(40)   Underlying form   Surface form

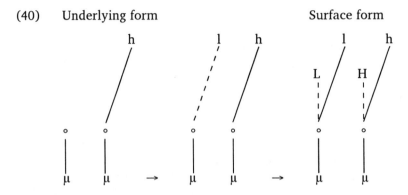

Example (40) represents a "minimal" system in which *h* register contrasts with its absence in underlying forms for any given TBU. Later, TBUs that are unspecified for register are assigned *l* register by default. Later still, the tonal feature *H* is assigned by default to TBUs associated to *h*, and the tonal feature *L* to TBUs associated to *l*. These tonal features serve to "enhance" the primary distinction between the higher register and the lower register, in keeping with the Enhancement Theory of Stevens and Keyser (1989) and Stevens et al. (1986).

The foregoing discussion accounts for why register features should be specified before tonal features, but it does not account for why in a surface two-tone system like (40) *h* is contrasted with its absence, as opposed to *l* being contrasted with its absence. While floating low tones are "marked" and need to be specified in underlying forms, cross-linguistically, low tones that are associated to segments are typically "unmarked" and serve as default tones. An example of this can be seen in the behavior of toneless morphemes. Although toneless morphemes often assimilate to the Hi tones of adjacent morphemes, in the absence of any such stimuli, they are typically realized with default Lo tones. It follows that if the Lo tone of a surface two-tone system is unmarked, the Hi tone must be marked and therefore specified in underlying forms. The marked nature of Hi tones may further be seen in that cross-linguistically, it is the Hi tone that typically spreads, as opposed to the Lo tone spreading.

Although systems like (40) are common for surface two-tone languages (e.g., Luganda, Odden 1988b), systems like (41) are also common for surface two-tone languages (e.g., Zulu, Clark 1988).

(41)   Underlying form   Surface form

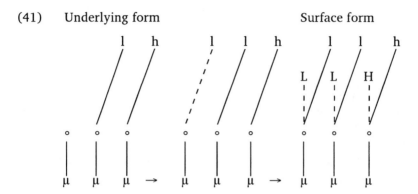

In this system, Hi contrasts with Lo and with toneless TBUs, with Lo tone typically associating to toneless TBUs by default.

Three-tone systems have two options for Mid tone. One is Mid$_1$ (tonal feature H and register feature l), and the other is Mid$_2$ (tonal feature L and register feature h). There are, of course, two ways to underspecify each of these two options, i.e., underlying register feature and default tonal feature, or underlying tonal feature and default register feature, but at this point in time it is not clear whether both options are actually found in natural languages. The derivation in (42) is assumed in chapter 6 for the three-tone (Mid$_1$) Acatlán Mixtec system.

(42)   a. Lo (toneless)

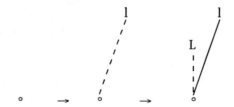

b. Mid   c. Hi

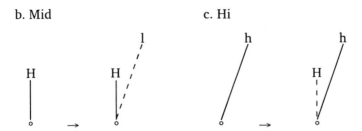

In (42), a TBU is either specified for *h* register, or it is unspecified for register. If it is unspecified for register, it receives *l* by default. It is also either specified for *H* tone, or it is unspecified for tone. If it is unspecified for tone, it receives *H* by default if the register is *h*, and *L* by default if the register is *l*, in keeping with the Enhancement Theory already mentioned.

2.5 Obligatory Contour Principle (OCP)

As stated in chapter 1, the OCP is not considered to be a universal constraint, but rather a cover term for a set of principles that conspire in many languages to prohibit the occurrence of adjacent identical features on nonskeletal tiers (cf. Odden 1986, 1988a and McCarthy 1986). In general, OCP effects are nearly universal within morphemes, but much less universal across morpheme boundaries. This means that for most languages, one does not find identical tones adjacent to one another within single morphemes. Monomorphemic forms like the Mende noun *bèlè* 'trousers', therefore, do not have two Lo tones, but rather one Lo tone that is associated to two TBUs. It is often the case, however, that like tones are placed in juxtaposition across word and morpheme boundaries. Left "unrepaired," this of course would violate the OCP. In these cases, languages are somewhat ideosyncratic in whether and to what extent the OCP holds at these derivational levels.

Tonal languages typically employ two main strategies in order to make derived surface forms conform to the OCP. The first strategy is simply to delete one or the other of the offending tones, and the second is to merge the two tones.

The deletion strategy often gives rise to what has been called *Meeussen's Rule,* named after the first linguist to recognize the phenomenon. Meeussen noticed that in many Bantu languages, stem-initial Hi tones changed to Lo when they followed certain Hi-toned clitics. This rule can also be stated as a deletion of the second of the two Hi tones, followed by the insertion of a default Lo tone. The examples in (43) illustrate Meeussen's Rule.

(43)   Shona (adapted from Kenstowicz 1994:325 and Odden 1980)

a.	mbwá	'dog'	né # mbwà	'with a dog'
b.	hóvé	'fish'	né # hòvè	'with a fish'
c.	bàdzá	'hoe'	né # bàdzá	'with a hoe'

In (43a), the Hi tone of *mbwá* is deleted and replaced with a default Lo tone when it follows Hi-toned *né*. In (43b), not only is the Hi tone of the first TBU of *hóvé* replaced with Lo tone, but the Hi tone of both TBUs is replaced. This clearly argues in favor of there being only one Hi tone that is underlyingly associated to both TBUs of *hóvé*. This single Hi tone is then deleted and the two TBUs to which it was associated are assigned Lo tone by default. Example (43c) was included in order to show that the phenomenon in question is not that of "polar tones." When a morpheme has a polar tone, it is consistently realized as the opposite to whatever is adjacent to it. In the case of (43c), the first TBU of *bàdzá* does not become Hi-toned when it follows *né*. The deletion strategy can, however, also give rise to polar tones. Compare these next examples.

(44)   Chumburung (personal data)

Singular	Plural	
jònò	í-jónô	'dog'
kísî	ì-kísî	'fetish'

In (44), the plural noun class prefix *i-* has a polar tone. When it precedes Lo-toned stems like *jònò*, the prefix is realized with a Hi tone that then spreads onto the stem. However, when it precedes a Hi-toned stem like *kísî*, it is realized as Lo tone. This prefix is analyzed as underlyingly bearing Hi tone. The Hi tone is then deleted and replaced with a default Lo tone when it precedes a stem that begins with Hi tone.[18] The effect of these processes is similar to that of Meeussen's Rule. In this case, however, it is the first of the two Hi tones that undergoes the change, as opposed to it being the second Hi, as in the case of Meeussen's Rule.

---

[18]In chapter 4, I analyze the process as deleting a register feature *h*, as opposed to a full Hi tone.

The second, and more common, strategy for repairing would-be OCP violations is for the two tones to simply merge or coalesce. In languages and environments in which Merger "applies," it does so after feature-filling default rules have applied, and assures that adjacent identical features, whether associated or not, are merged into one. In these languages, it fails to merge identical features only when there is an intervening nonidentical feature present on the same tier. In the case studies that follow, most of the languages provide no reason to think that the OCP does not apply. By the same token, however, Acatlán Mixtec provides no reason to think that it does apply and good reason to think that it does not. Since the merger strategy plays a crucial role in the present work, a number of hypothetical inputs are presented in order to illustrate how it does apply in languages in which it is invoked.

(45)

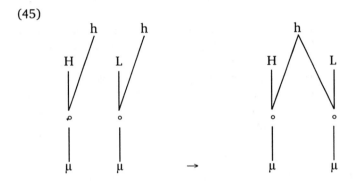

In (45), even though the tonal features of the two TBUs are not identical, the two register *hs* are merged because they are identical and are adjacent.

(46)

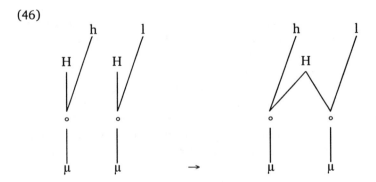

The situation in (46) is the same as that in (45), except that in (46) it is the tonal features that are merged instead of the register features.

(47)

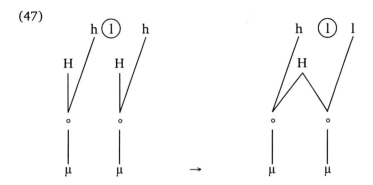

In (47), even though the features associated to the two TBUs are identical, only the tonal features merge. Merger is blocked in the case of the register *hs* because there is an intervening floating register *l*.

(48)

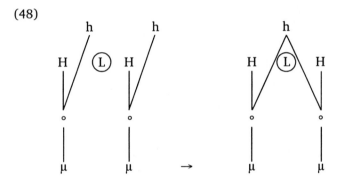

The situation in (48) is the same as that in (47), except that in (48) it is the register features that are merged instead of the tonal features.

Merger also coalesces TRNs that dominate identical feature specifications. If even one specification is different, however, as in (49d), this does not take place.

(49)   a.

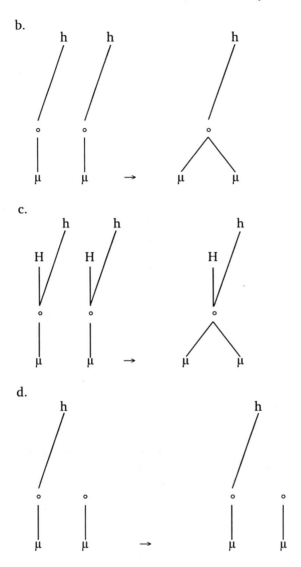

This closes the treatment of the theoretical model. In the following chapters we demonstrate the explanatory potential of the model and then examine a number of case studies that employ RTT. Before doing this, however, it is worth summarizing the roles played by the various phonological principles discussed in this chapter. The first concerns default feature specifications. I assume that default values for features that contrast in underlying forms are filled in prior to those for features which do not contrast in underlying forms. I also assume that the Obligatory Contour Principle (OCP) is not a universal constraint, but rather a cover term for a set of principles that conspire in many languages to prohibit the occurrence of adjacent identical features on nonskeletal tiers. For languages and environments in which Merger applies, it does so after feature-filling default rules have applied and assures that adjacent identical features, whether associated or not, are merged into one. In these languages, it fails to merge identical features only when there is an intervening nonidentical feature present on the same tier.

A claim made in Snider (1990a) is that a rule of Stray Erasure, or pruning, empirically well-motivated for nontonal phenomena (cf. Itô 1986), applies at the end of the postlexical component to delete all unassociated tonal features prior to the application of any phonetic, i.e., gradient feature component, rules. This means that only features which are associated, i.e., prosodically licensed, at the end of the phonology component play a role in the phonetics component.[19] Finally, it is generally assumed that following all phonological "activity," an algorithm in the phonetics component interprets the representations that have been output from the phonology component. Throughout the remainder of this book, these principles are assumed to apply in the following order: (1) feature-filling default rules, (2) Merger (if it applies), (3) Stray Erasure, and (4) phonetic algorithm.

---

[19]Crucially, Merger does not apply after Stray Erasure.

3
Explanatory Potential of the Model

The preceding chapter presented a "bare-bones" outline of the geometry and features of the model without attempting to provide a rationale for what was presented. In this chapter, we look at what the model can "do." As stated in the introduction, a model for the representation of tone must be able to uniquely represent each tone phoneme in any given language, account for the different types of tonal alternations found in natural language, and adequately characterize the different types of contour tones found in natural language. With this in mind, we consider in the abstract a number of common tonal phenomena, with a view to exploring the explanatory potential of the model. Not all that the model can do is yet attested; however, this chapter demonstrates something of the range of phenomena that are possible.

3.1 Assimilations

Recall that in autosegmental phonology, assimilation processes are represented by spreading rules. This includes both total assimilations and partial assimilations. Recall also that spreading rules can apply either from left to right or from right to left. Total assimilations are represented in RTT by spreading from nodes on the TRN tier to moras on the TBU tier. A very typical total assimilation for tone is that of Hi-Tone Spreading (HTS).

(50)   a. HTS in Chumburung

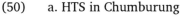

ká jònò   →   [ká jónò]   'wife's dog'

b. Structural representation   Phonetic representation

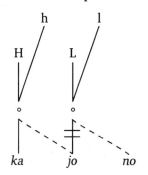 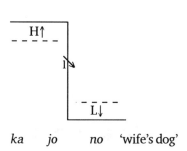

ka   jo   no   ka   jo   no   'wife's dog'

In the Structural Representation of (50b), the tonal phoneme *Hi*, represented by the tonal feature *H* and the register feature *h* (conjoined on the TRN tier), spreads rightwards from the first tonal root node, on the TRN tier, to the second TBU, on the TBU tier. In a separate process, the tonal phoneme *Lo* is delinked from that second TBU, due to a constraint in the language that disallows a contour tone in this environment. In the phonetic representation, both *ka* and *jo* are phonetically realized on the same register and tone and are consequently realized with the same pitch.

As noted above, partial assimilations are represented by spreading between either the Tonal tier and the TRN tier, or the Register tier and the TRN tier. The following Ewe example (from Stahlke 1971) illustrates the partial assimilation of a Lo tone to Mid before Hi.

(51)   a. Mid tone creation in Ewe

ŋyìlá   →   [ŋyī lá]   'the cow'

b. Structural representation   Phonetic representation

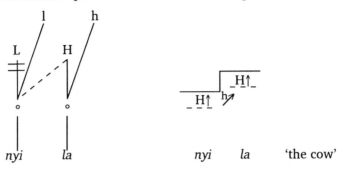

nyi   la   nyi   la   'the cow'

In (51) the tonal feature H of the Hi-toned lá spreads leftwards onto the
TRN of the Lo-toned nyì. The original tonal feature L of the Lo tone is
delinked in a separate process, similar to that in the preceding
Chumburung example. This results in the underlying Lo tone being realized as a surface Mid. The fact that the Lo is realized as Mid instead of Hi
indicates that the assimilation is only partial, and that the first TBU did not
assimilate to all of the Hi tone's features.

The second type of partial assimilation is represented by spreading between the Register tier and the TRN tier. Downstep is probably the most
common example of this in African languages. As mentioned in chapter 1,
downstep is of two varieties: automatic and nonautomatic (Stewart 1965,
1983). A language has automatic downstep when the following conditions
are met: (a) the Lo of a Hi Lo sequence is realized on a lower register than
the preceding Hi (cf. 52a), and (b) the Hi of a Lo Hi sequence is realized on
the same register as the preceding Lo (cf. 52b).

(52)   Automatic downstep

        a. Hi Lo sequence   b. Lo Hi sequence

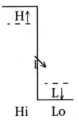

        Hi   Lo   Lo   Hi

c. Hi Lo Hi sequence

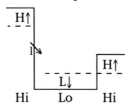

Hi   Lo   Hi

The actual downstepped sequence begins with the Lo. When these conditions are met, the second Hi of a Hi Lo Hi sequence (cf. 52c) is realized with a lower pitch than the first. Nonautomatic downstep differs from automatic downstep only in that the Lo is unassociated, or floating, in nonautomatic downstep.[20] The following example illustrates both (nonautomatic) downstep and HTS in Chumburung.

(53)   a. Downstep in Chumburung

     náátí kìsíbɔ́   →   [náátí kíʼsíbɔ́]   'cow's ear'

     b. Structural representation   Phonetic representation

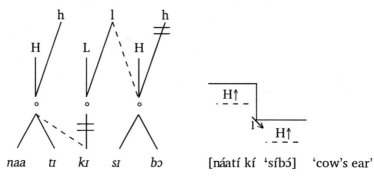

naa   tɪ   kɪ   sɪ   bɔ   [náátí kí ʼsíbɔ́]   'cow's ear'

In (53), the TBUs are associated to the following features in their input forms: naa (H, h), tɪ (H, h), kɪ (L, l), sɪ (H, h), and bɔ (H, h). Subsequently,

---

[20]I am using Stewart's terminology in order to avoid some of the confusion that exists in the literature with regard to pitch lowering phenomena. Other terms include: "downdrift" (Anderson 1978) to describe automatic downstep, "downstep" (Anderson 1978) to describe nonautomatic downstep, "catathesis" (Poser 1984, Beckman and Pierrehumbert 1986) to describe downstep phenomena in general, "declination" (Ladd 1984) to describe the general tendency for pitch to decline gradually over the course of an utterance, even when all tones in the utterance are identical, and "downtrend" (Connell and Ladd 1990:2) to describe "any overall lowering of speaking pitch during the course of an utterance."

the rule of HTS applies, just as in (50). In addition, there is spreading between the *l* on the Register tier to the TRN of the underlyingly Hi-toned *síbɔ́*. The original *h* of that word is delinked, with the result that the Hi tone of *síbɔ́* is realized on the lower register of the preceding Lo tone. This results in the TBUs being associated to the following features in their surface, or output forms: *naa* (H, h), *tɩ* (H, h), *kɩ* (H, h), *sɩ* (H, l), and *bɔ* (H, l).[21]

So far, we have looked only at cases in which spreading directly to the target results in well-formed paths; e.g., when the argument is a register or tone feature, the target is a TRN, or when the argument is a TRN, the target is a TBU. As we will see in later chapters, it is sometimes the case that when the argument is a register or tone feature, the target needs to be a TBU. Consider the situation in (54) in which a register feature *h* is underlyingly associated to a TRN that is, in turn, associated to two TBUs. If the target of the *l*-Spread rule is the TRN, then it automatically follows that application of the rule will result in the *l* affecting both of the TBUs that were originally associated to the *h*.

(54)   Target of *l*-Spread: TRN

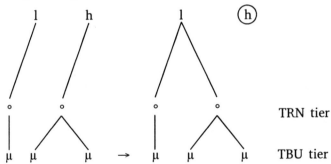

But it is occasionally the case that the spreading of a feature affects only the first TBU. When this happens, we say that the target of the spreading rule is the TBU, instead of the TRN. Since features associate only to TRNs and not directly to TBUs, spreading directly to the target in a case like this would create an ill-formed path. In order to avoid the creation of an ill-formed path, it is first necessary to split the TRN that is associated to the target TBU so that the target TBU has its own TRN. This is accomplished

---

[21]In this discussion of (53), I have provided input and output feature specifications for each TBU. This was done in order to help orient the reader to correctly interpreting the structural representation. Because this wrongly implies that adjacent TBUs that are associated to the same features have separate feature specifications, I will not normally follow this practice in describing representations throughout this work.

through a process called Tonal Root Node Fission,[22] which generates the appropriate structure to ensure well-formedness.

(55)   Target of l-Spread: TBU

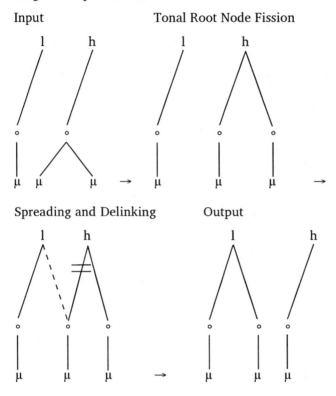

In (55), the target of the l-Spread rule is the TBU, and so the rightmost node splits, allowing the l register feature to spread to the new TRN and delink the h that was associated to it. This can be contrasted with the more normal case of (54), in which the target of the l-Spread rule is the TRN itself, and the node does not split.

---

[22]The notion of node fission was first proposed in Clements (1989) and has since been exploited in such works as Clements and Hume (1995) and Schane (1995).

3.2 Downstep and upstep

From the preceding section it can be seen that downstep of Hi tone occurs when the second of two Hi-tones assimilates to the lower register of
an adjacent Lo tone. By exploiting the model of tonal geometry assumed in
this work, and making certain assumptions regarding boundary tones (discussed next), it is possible to generate a four-way typology of downstep
systems. At this point in time, it is not yet known whether or not this
typology is valid. However, it accounts in a unified manner for a number
of seemingly disparate register phenomena in (at least) the Niger-Congo
family of African languages, and it is set forth here more as an interesting
idea to be tested than anything else.

Although the concept of boundary tones is relatively new to linguists, it is
not a particularly surprising phenomenon, given what is already known
about floating tones and clitics. One normally thinks of floating tones as being associated with certain words, i.e., certain words are known to begin or
end in floating tones. One also thinks of floating tones as sole morphemes in
their own right, morphemes that historically have lost their segmental at-
tributes and consist solely of floating tones. In African languages, tonal morphemes often serve as noun class markers and tense/aspect markers. With
respect to clitics, clitics are particles that attach themselves to no particular
class of morphemes or words, but rather are found at the edges, or boundaries, of certain syntactic constituents, regardless of how long those constituents may be. One can think of boundary tones as simply clitics that consist
solely of floating tones. The examples in (56) illustrate a Lo boundary tone
(BT) in Bimoba that is consistently assigned to the right edge of the noun
phrase, regardless of the length of the phrase (data from Snider 1998).

(56)   Bimoba (Ghana)

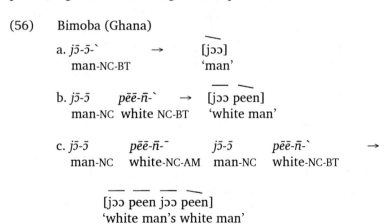

Throughout the examples in (56), all tones, including the floating Mid associative marker (AM) in (56c), are Mid, except for the floating Lo boundary tone. This Lo tone docks onto the final syllable of the noun phrase, where it combines with, in the case of the examples in (56), the lexical Mid tone and is realized as a Mid-falling tone.

In order to account for the wide variety of seemingly disparate register phenomena mentioned above, I first propose that phonological phrases in many if not all Niger-Congo languages have Lo boundary tones assigned to their left and right edges. The notion that there is a floating Lo at the right edge of phrases finds support in the fact that phrase-final Lo tones are falling in most Niger-Congo languages. Motivation for a boundary tone at the left edge of phrases finds support in languages like Engenni (see chapter 5). The super Hi tones of many of these languages are more easily analyzed if one assumes that there is a boundary tone at the left edge of their phrases. The fact that languages with super Hi tones are quite common in the Niger-Congo family suggests that phrase-edge boundary tone phenomenon may very well be a characteristic of the family. How these boundary tones interact with the other tones of the phrase will become apparent below. Secondly, I propose that there are two parameters at play—the direction in which *l*s spread, and the domain of the spread. Spreading in autosegmental theory is either iterative or noniterative (cf. chapter 1, this volume, and Archangeli and Pulleyblank 1994). In the case of downstep, the spreading of *l* is always iterative, that is, the *l*-Spread rule continues to reapply to its output until its structural description is no longer met. In other words, rather than simply spreading to one (i.e., the first) target, the *l* spreads to the entire string of eligible targets. The domain, however, is restricted in certain languages. The two parameters, Direction (Right/Left) and Domain (Restricted/Nonrestricted), generate a four-way typology.

For those languages in which the domain of *l*-Spread is nonrestricted, *l* spreads iteratively either leftwards or rightwards, and delinks any adjacent *h*s that are associated to its target TRNs. In this case, any adjacent *h*s are set floating. For those languages in which the domain is restricted, *l* spreads in the same manner as for those languages in which the domain is nonrestricted except for the following constraint. Spreading is not permitted to cause an adjacent *h* to float if there is another *l* following the *h*. The *l* therefore spreads to all but the last eligible TRN. Stating the constraint more technically, a floating *h* register feature may not occur between associated *l* register features. One can also say that the constraint prevents two *l* register features from being associated to adjacent TBUs. For rightward spreading, if there is a Lo tone following the Hi, the *l* spreads to all TRNs but one and delinks the *h* that was underlyingly associated to them. If there is no Lo tone following the Hi (i.e., the Hi is utterance-final), the *l* spreads to all TRNs, i.e., the domain of the downstep is nonrestricted. The mirror-image of this holds for leftward spreading.

The difference between the restricted and nonrestricted types of *l* spreading, and between the leftwards and rightwards types of *l* spreading is shown in these next examples. In order to keep the structural representations of these examples as uncluttered as possible, complete derivations and boundary *l*s are shown only for (57). In the examples that follow (57), the boundary *l*s are inserted only when they play a role in the derivation. It will be kept in mind, however, that the proposal assumes that they are always at the left and right edges of phonological phrases, even when their presence is redundant. Throughout these next examples, Delink applies after *l*-Spread, although the two are shown in the same structural representations for the sake of economy. Also, in order to keep digression to a minimum, only automatic downstep will be shown.

When the spreading is nonrestricted and rightward, as in (57), it results in the normal terracing downstep that is common to many African languages.

(57)   Domain: Nonrestricted; Direction: Right

       a. Utterance begins with Lo

       Input   Merger, *l*-Spread and Delink

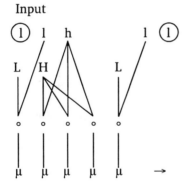   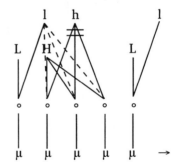

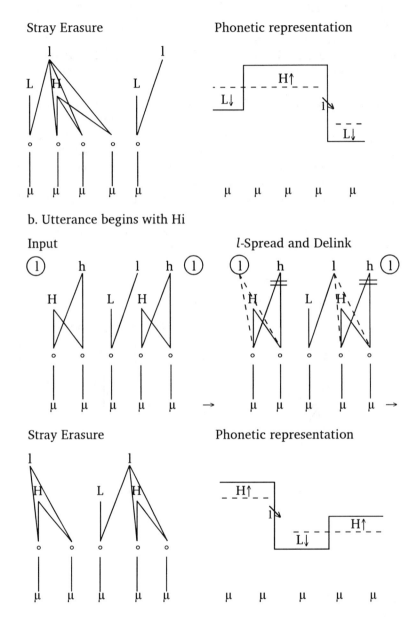

In (57), the leftmost and rightmost *l*s are boundary tones and are circled to indicate that they are floating. Following the principles outlined at the end of chapter 2, at the end of the phonological derivation, all floating features are deleted by Stray Erasure. As one can see in both examples of (57), the downstep effect is "terrace-like," so that the tonal register descends in a series of steps, and once lowered, is never again raised within the same phonological phrase. It is also the case that all adjacent like tones are realized at the same level. Rightward spreading in which the domain is nonrestricted is illustrated by the Chumburung data in chapter 4.

When the spreading is restricted and rightward, as in (58), it results in downstep followed by a nondownstepped Hi.

(58)   Domain: Restricted; Direction: Right

a. Utterance begins with Lo

Structural representation   Phonetic representation

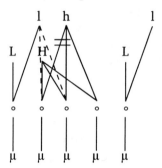
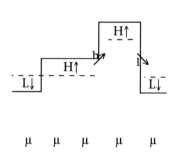

b. Utterance begins with Hi

Structural representation   Phonetic representation

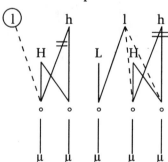
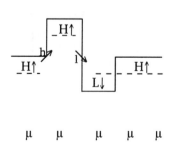

Notice that at the left edge of (58b), the *l* that spreads is the left boundary tone. In the case of (58a), the boundary tone is not shown because it is assumed to have merged with the leftmost *l* of the utterance. As for the right boundary tone, it is not shown in either case because with rightward spreading, its presence would make no difference to the phonetic representations. Notice also that whereas the leftmost *l* spreads two moras in (58a), it spreads only one mora in (58b). This is because when the domain of the spreading is restricted, it spreads to all but the final mora, regardless of how many eligible moras are in the string. Finally, notice in (58b) that whereas the leftmost *l* spreads to the last but one eligible mora, the rightmost *l* spreads in a nonrestricted manner to *all* of the eligible moras. Spreading of the leftmost *l* is restricted to the last but one eligible mora in the string because spreading further would violate the constraint against the occurrence of a floating *h* between associated *l*s. But in the case of the rightmost *l*, the spreading is nonrestricted because spreading to all of the eligible moras in the string does not produce this violation. In this case, although the *h* is set floating, it is does not violate the constraint because the *h* does not float between associated *l*s. Rightward spreading in which the domain is restricted is illustrated by the Engenni data in chapter 5.

When the domain is restricted and the spreading is leftward, as in (59), it results in "nondownstep" followed by downstep.

(59)   Domain: Restricted; Direction: Left

        a. Utterance begins with Lo

        Structural representation   Phonetic representation

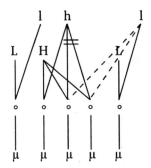   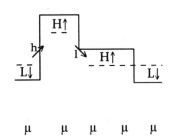

b. Utterance begins with Hi

Structural representation   Phonetic representation

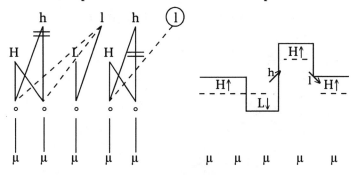

Notice again that at the right edges of (59b) and (60b), the *l* that spreads is the boundary tone. Since (59) is the mirror image of (58), the discussion of (58) may prove helpful in interpreting (59). One language that has leftward spreading in which the domain is restricted is Krachi. Although the RTT analysis of Krachi that is presented in Snider 1990a recognizes the super Hi tone as "upstepped," the analysis presented easily lends itself to one along the lines suggested here.

When the domain of *l*-Spread is nonrestricted and the spreading is leftward, as in (60), the result is what could be called "total" downstep. Notice that this type of downstep is also terracing. At this point in time, I am not aware of any language that has a downstep system like this. Although languages like Kikuyu are also total downstep systems, the Kikuyu system is quite different from that of (60).

(60)   Domain: Nonrestricted; Direction: Left

    a. Utterance begins with Lo

Structural representation   Phonetic representation

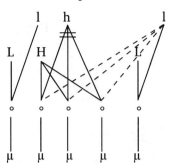   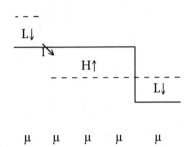

    b. Utterance begins with Hi

Structural representation   Phonetic representation

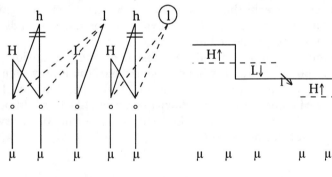

    Notice that in order for the level of the downstepped Hi to be the same as the level of the preceding Lo tone, it is necessary to assume a ratio of 1/1 for the register/tone feature values. This point is dealt with at length in §3.4. The four-way typology generated by the two parameters, Direction (Right/Left) and Domain (Restricted/Nonrestricted) is summarized in (61).

(61)   A typology of downstep

	Direction: Right	Direction: Left
Domain: Nonrestricted	Terracing downstep (e.g., Chumburung)	Total downstep
Domain: Restricted	Nonterracing downstep type 1 (e.g., Engenni)	Nonterracing downstep type 2 (e.g., Krachi)

Although the discussion so far has focussed primarily on automatic downstep (i.e., downstep that is attributable to associated Lo tones), the reader has been introduced to the notion of nonautomatic downstep (i.e., downstep when the Lo tone that conditions it is floating). It is also the case that floating Lo tones can trigger upstep. In fact, RTT predicts that downstep and upstep of *any* tone can be triggered by any floating tone, provided the register of the floating tone is of opposite value to the tone that undergoes the downstep or upstep.[23] Examples (62)–(65) present some of the logical possibilities for such a tone.

(62)   a. Downstep of Hi   b. Upstep of Hi

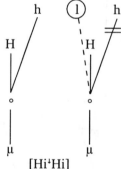

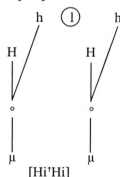

[Hi'Hi]   [Hi'Hi]

In (62a), the floating *l* spreads rightwards onto the third Tonal Root Node (TRN) and the original *h* associated with that node is dissociated. Consequently, the pitch of the second TBU is downstepped relative to the first TBU. Technically, the point of downstep is between the Hi and Lo

---

[23]Although not the focus of this paper, empirical evidence to support these "additional" predictions comes from descriptions of Mids that undergo downstep (Elugbe 1986, Newman 1971, Van der Kolk 1992), and of Mids that cause Hi's to be downstepped (Armstrong 1968 and Snider 1998).

tones, and the downstepped Hi has "assimilated" to the register of the Lo. In (62b), the floating l does not spread, but remains floating. In RTT, only features that are associated at the end of the phonological derivation play a role in the phonetics component because all floating features are deleted at the end of the phonological derivation by Stray Erasure. As a result, although both TBUs have Hi tone, the second is upstepped relative to the first because it is associated to a distinct h. Notice that Merger does not prohibit there being distinct hs associated to these adjacent TBUs since on the Register tier there is an intervening l.

     Example (62) demonstrates the effect of a floating l in causing downstep and upstep of Hi; (63)–(65) similarly demonstrate the effect of floating tones in causing downstep and upstep of the two types of Mid tones introduced in chapter 2, and of Lo.

(63)   a. Downstep of M_1 b. Upstep of M_1

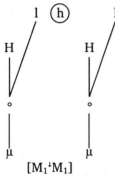 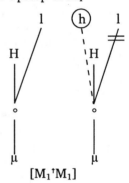

$[M_1\text{'}M_1]$ $[M_1\text{'}M_1]$

(64)   a. Downstep of M_2 b. Upstep of M_2

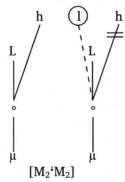 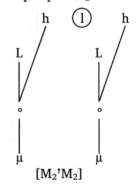

$[M_2\text{'}M_2]$ $[M_2\text{'}M_2]$

(65)   a. Downstep of Lo   b. Upstep of Lo

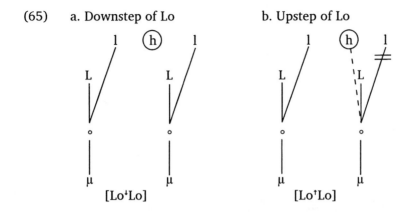

          [Lo'Lo]   [Lo'Lo]

In each of these examples, one of the phenomena (downstep or upstep) occurs when the floating register feature stays floating, and the opposite phenomenon occurs when the floating register feature spreads rightwards.

3.3 Contour tones

We next explore the different options RTT sanctions for representing the different types of contour tones found in natural language. Yip (1989) describes contour tones as being of two main types: composite contours, which function primarily as phonological sequences of two or more level tones, and unitary contours, which function primarily as phonological units (we discuss these differences further below). Although contours of the latter variety do function as units, the beginning and end points of these contours can be equated with certain level tones in the language. The geometry of RTT permits one to represent both composite and unitary contours in a manner that respects their composite and unitary natures. (66) and (67) show the three possible representations of Hi-falling contours allowed for in the model.

(66)   Composite contour

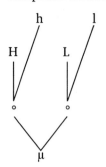

(67)   Unitary contours

        a. Change in register   b. Change in tone

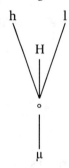   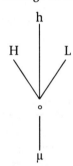

In the case of a composite contour tone, the features are dominated by two (or more, in principle) tonal root nodes associated to a single TBU. In the case of a unitary contour, the features are dominated by a single tonal root node associated to a single TBU. There are two types of unitary contours predicted by the model: (a) those that involve a change in register and (b) those that involve a change in tone on a given register. Whether both types of contours are actually exploited in natural languages, however, is the subject of ongoing investigation.

Composite contours and unitary contours differ in at least two respects. First, whereas unitary contours appear to be as freely distributed on the TBUs of morphemes as level tones, composite contours appear to be realized mainly on edges. This reflects their historical development. Many composite contours are the result of historical loss in which a TBU at the edge of a word or morpheme is deleted. When this happens, the tone of the deleted TBU normally remains, and often associates to the new edge TBU where it may join with another (different) tone to form a composite contour. Other composite contours are the result of spreading a level tone from one word or morpheme to the edge TBU of an adjacent word or morpheme, where it joins with the existing level tone of that second word or morpheme. Composite and unitary contours also differ in the ways they spread and reduplicate. Whereas composite contours can only spread and reduplicate one or other of their composite parts to adjacent TBUs, as illustrated in (68a), unitary contours are claimed (Yip 1989, Chan 1991) to spread and reduplicate as units to adjacent TBUs, as illustrated in (68b).

(68)   a. Spreading from composite contour

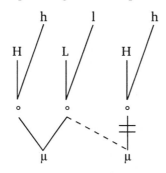

b. Spreading from unitary contour

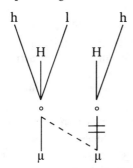

3.4 Multiple tone heights

In chapter 2, emphasis was placed on defining the features that are used to represent tone, and little was said concerning the relative contribution each feature makes to the overall pitch height of any given TBU. One can think of this relative difference in terms of a register/tone ratio that is specific for each language. The register/tone ratio is defined as the ratio of the phonetic difference attributable to moving from one register level to another when the tone is the same compared to the phonetic difference attributable to moving from one tone to another when the register is the same. Languages differ in this regard. In some languages, the phonetic difference attributable to moving from one register level to another is less than that attributable to moving from one tone to another on a given register. In other languages, they are equal. This is demonstrated below.

Look at (69), repeated from chapter 2.

(69)   a.   b.   c.   d.

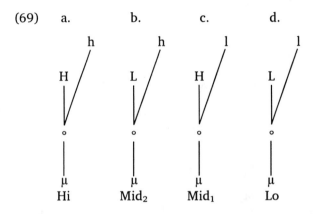

In (69), four tone phonemes are represented. However, if these representations are to characterize four different pitch heights (as opposed to three), one needs to assume that the difference in pitch attributable to a change in register is not equal to the difference in pitch attributable to a change in tone on the tonal tier. To show why this is so, we examine two types of tone systems.

In (70) we assume that any increase or decrease in pitch due to shifts in tonal register is *less than* any increase or decrease in pitch due to changes in tone from L to H, or from H to L, respectively. Specifically for (70), we assume that every upward or downward shift in register increases or decreases, respectively, the relative numerical value of the overall pitch (indicated by the numerals under each representation) by a factor of one. We also assume that every change in tone from L to H, or from H to L increases or decreases, respectively, the relative numerical value of the overall pitch by a factor of two. So we say, then, that the register/tone ratio for the representations in (70) is 1/2. This allows one to represent up to four relative heights. The numerical value of the overall pitch for the first TBU of each representation (always Lo tone) is arbitrarily set at 1. The numerical value for the second TBU is computed by assuming a value of $+1$ for each increase in pitch called for by the register features, and a value of $+2$ for each increase in pitch called for by the tonal features.

(70)   a. Lo Lo with register/tone ratio of 1/2

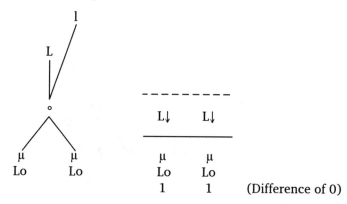

(Difference of 0)

b. Lo Mid$_2$ with register/tone ratio of 1/2

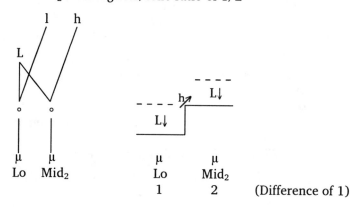

(Difference of 1)

c. Lo Mid$_1$ with register/tone ratio of 1/2

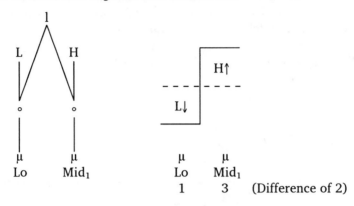

	μ	μ	
	Lo	Mid$_1$	
	1	3	(Difference of 2)

d. Lo Hi with register/tone ratio of 1/2

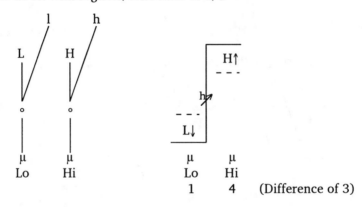

	μ	μ	
	Lo	Hi	
	1	4	(Difference of 3)

Now compare (70) with (71), which has a register/tone ratio of 1/1.

(71)   a. Lo Lo with register/tone ratio of 1/1

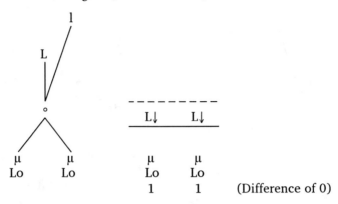

(Difference of 0)

b. Lo Mid$_2$ with register/tone ratio of 1/1

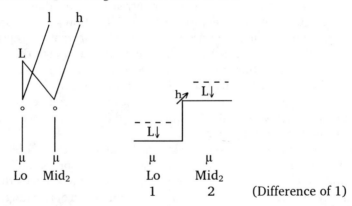

(Difference of 1)

c. Lo Mid$_1$ with register/tone ratio of 1/1

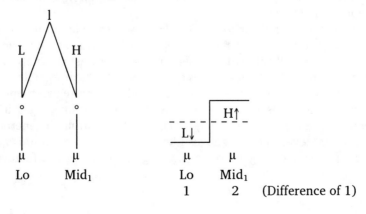

(Difference of 1)

d. Lo Hi with register/tone ratio of 1/1

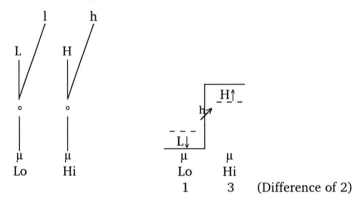

In (71) we assume that any increase or decrease in pitch due to shifts in tonal register is *equal to* any increase or decrease in pitch due to changes in tone. Notice that whereas the ratio of 1/2 in (70) allows us to represent up to four relative heights, the ratio of 1/1 in (71) allows us to represent no more than three relative heights. This means that although the structural representations for Mid$_1$ and Mid$_2$ are *phonologically* distinct, they are not *phonetically* distinct. In (70) and (71), the ratios used were 1/2, and 1/1, respectively. The whole numbers of the first ratio, of course, were chosen for illustrative purposes only. In actual fact, the precise ratio employed by any one language is language-specific.

So far, we have discussed cases in which the phonetic difference attributable to the difference between *l* and *h* is "less than" or "equal to" that attributable to the difference between *L* and *H*. There also exists the logical possibility of "greater than." Although I am not aware of any languages for which this is in fact the case, we would expect a downstepped Hi tone in a four-level tone language to be lower than the second highest tone, should languages like this exist.

The features and geometry of RTT as presented so far allow one to fully specify up to four level tone phonemes: Hi, Mid$_1$, Mid$_2$, and Lo. The model, however, is actually able to represent up to six contrastive levels following any given tone. (72) demonstrates the six levels that are possible following a M$_1$ tone. In these examples I have inserted floating register features between certain tones in order to show that even in languages in which Merger applies (perhaps the majority), it is still possible to generate up to six different levels. For languages like this, the floating features have the effect of blocking Merger from coalescing identical register features. And for languages in which Merger is not invoked, the floating features of these examples would have no effect.

(72)

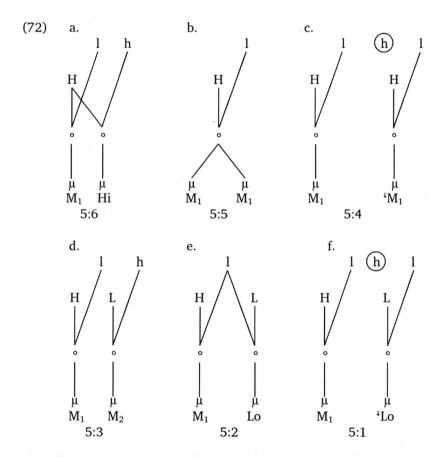

In (72), I have arbitrarily assigned a phonetic value of 5 to the first TBU of each pair. The value for the second TBU was computed by assuming a value of $+1$ or -1, respectively, for each raising or lowering of the tonal register called for by the register features, and a value of $+3$ or -3, respectively, for each raising or lowering of tone called for by the tonal features.

In response to the claim that the present proposal can generate more than four contrastive levels of tone, it might be argued that the model, in fact, is able to represent up to *twelve* contrasting levels: Hi, M_2, M_1, Lo; $^!$Hi, $^!M_2$, $^!M_1$, $^!$Lo; and $^+$Hi, $^+M_2$, $^+M_1$, $^+$Lo. This is only an illusion, however. It is *not* possible to generate twelve after any *given* level. An upstepped Hi, for instance, cannot be generated following a M_1. Similarly, a downstepped M_2 cannot be generated following a Lo. It is also the case that many of the twelve tones listed actually represent the same level. An upstepped Lo, for example, is structurally equivalent to M_2, and a downstepped Hi is structurally equivalent to M_1. This also explains why certain representations (e.g., $M_1{}^!M_1$) appear to be missing from (72). The apparent omissions are structurally equivalent to other representations. In the case of $M_1{}^!M_1$, it is identical to M_1Hi. Following any given tone, the maximum number of levels possible is only six.

While cases can be made for establishing up to four contrastive pitch levels (i.e., Hi, M_1, M_2, and Lo) in natural language, clear cases for more than four levels are much harder to come by. Two of the clearest, however, are Longacre's (1952) description of five levels in Trique (Mexico), and Flik's (1977) description of five levels in Dan (Côte d'Ivoire). I analyze the fifth level of Trique as Super Hi (equatable with upstepped Hi), and the fifth level of Dan as Super Lo (equatable with downstepped Lo).

(73)   a. Trique   b. Dan

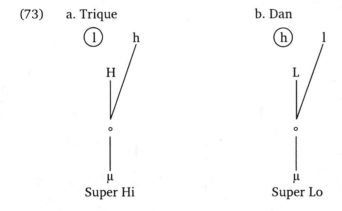

Since the fifth level is phonemic in each case, it must be given a unique underlying representation. In order to do this, models that employ the features of traditional generative phonology must add a third binary feature to the system (with the accompanying problems of overgeneration). With the register features of the present model, however, this is not necessary.

The Super Hi or Super Lo tone of languages with five contrastive pitch levels is a complex structure, analogous to the "phonemic" contour tones found on monosyllabic morphemes in many African languages. Although the contour tones of Africa can be phonemic (in the sense that they contrast with other tones in analogous and identical environments), they are really concatenations of two or more other tones, and are properly represented as such in underlying forms. In a similar way, the Super Hi or Super Lo is a complex that involves a concatenation of two register features.[24] The complex tone consists of a floating register feature before an associated tone of opposite register value. This floating register feature has the effect of blocking Merger from coalescing otherwise identical adjacent register features.

One argument against the assumption that the fifth and sixth phonemic level tones are really "complex" tones is that the five or six levels can apparently be aurally distinguished even when they are spoken in isolation. If a Super Hi occurred only following a Hi tone, it would obviously not pose a problem for the present proposal since it could be upstepped relative to a preceding Hi tone. But a monosyllabic form in isolation does not have anything preceding it relative to which a Super Hi could be upstepped. Recall, however, the assumption stated above that native speakers begin all utterances with a reference point in mind. If this reference point were "Hi," the isolation form for a Super Hi complex would be upstepped relative to that reference point.

We turn now to consider four case studies that illustrate the explanatory power of the proposals made above.

---

[24]This is not to say that all descriptions of Super Hi's in the literature should be represented in this manner. Many of the "Super Hi" or "Extra Hi" tones in the literature are simply nonlowered Hi's that contrast with lowered Hi's (e.g., Engenni, chapter 5, this volume; and Mankon, cf., Leroy 1977 and Mfonyam 1988).

4

Terracing Downstep in Chumburung

4.1 Tone classes

Most nouns in Chumburung consist of a stem and one of six different noun class prefixes. Tonally, all prefixes behave identically. In addition, there are a few nouns (mostly referring to animals) which do not take a prefix in their singular forms. For monomorphemic CVCV noun stems, any given stem is assigned to one of four tonal classes. Following Casali's (1994) analysis of nominal tone in Nawuri, a language very closely related to Chumburung, I analyze all surface Lo tones in Chumburung as underlyingly unspecified for tone (toneless), with all surface Lo tones being assigned by default. The four tonal classes are shown in (74) and are labeled HH, HØ, ØH, and ØØ (where Ø = toneless, and HH is a single Hi associated to two TBUs).[25] Examples of these appear also in (74), where they are arranged in columns according to noun class.[26] Taking into account forms with prefixes and forms without prefixes, the four underlying melodies generate six different surface melodies, pairs like *kísî* and *kí-pínî, and tìrí* and *kì-síbɔ́* being considered to have the same surface melodies, i.e., Hi Lo and Lo Hi, respectively.

---

[25]Following Hyman (1992), I assume the TBU to be a mora (μ), either the head mora of the syllable, or the nonhead mora of the syllable if it dominates a [−Consonantal] root node.

[26]Chumburung has both cross-height vowel harmony, based on the feature *Advanced Tongue Root* (cf. Stewart and Van Leynseele 1979) and back/round vowel harmony. All harmony within words (but not across word boundaries) is represented in the data. In these data ɜ represents [+ ATR] a. For a description of these phenomena, see Snider (1989).

(74)   CVCV noun roots

	Gender 1			Gender 2		
Root Melody	Sing.	Pl.	Gloss	Sing.	Pl.	Gloss
HH	náatí	ì-náatí	'cow'	kì-síbɔ́	à-síbɔ́	'ear'
HØ	kísî	ì-kísî	'fetish'	kì-bújî	ɜ̀-bújî	'grindstone'
ØH	tìɪrí	ì-tìɪrí	'goat'	kù-kùtí	ɜ̀-kùtí	'orange'
ØØ	jònò	í-jónô	'dog'	kí-pínî	á-pínî	'mortar'

A cursory look at (74) reveals that whenever there is an underlying Hi in the stem, the prefix is Lo, and whenever the stem is underlyingly tone-less, the prefix is Hi. (Similar observations appear in Snider 1990b and Snider 1990c.) At this point the present analysis diverges slightly from that of Casali. Whereas Casali analyzes the prefix as underlyingly toneless (we return to this point below), I analyze the prefix as underlyingly bearing *h*. A lexical rule of *h*-Deletion, similar to *Meeussen's Rule* for Bantu (cf. Gold-smith 1984), deletes the prefix *h* whenever there is another *h* to its right.

(75)   h-Deletion (lexical)

   h → Ø / __ h

In addition to the forms of (74), there exist nouns like *kì-bwànɔ̀* 'tooth', in which all TBUs have surface Lo tone. Words like this are not plentiful and no clear-cut monomorphemic examples are known. I assume stems like this are the product of compounding (cf. *ká-nɔ́* 'mouth,' toneless root) in which at least one of the roots has a floating *h* that triggers the deletion of the prefix *h*.

A second lexical rule that applies is *l*-Assignment, which assigns an *l* by default to all toneless TRNs. This is formalized in (76).

(76)   *l*-Assignment (lexical)

The derivations in (77) demonstrate the application of *h*-Deletion and *l*-Assignment.

(77)   Underlying Form   *í-náatí*   *í-tʊrí*

        h-Deletion   *ɪ-náatí*   *ɪ-tʊrí*

        l-Assignment   *ì-náatí*   *ì-tɪrí*

        Surface Form   [ìnáatí]   'cows'   [ìtɪɪrí]   'goats'

As already stated, Casali (1994) analyzes the nominal prefix in Nawuri as underlyingly toneless. In order to account for those cases in which a surface Hi is realized, he proposes a lexical rule of Prefix Tone Assignment that assigns a Hi tone to all toneless prefixes. In order to account for those cases in which a surface Hi tone is not realized, he suggests, "the failure of Prefix Tone Assignment to apply to stems with the simple melody *H* is due to the Obligatory Contour Principle...which prohibits the occurrence of adjacent identical tones within the same word" (Casali 1994:54). A later rule assigns a default Lo tone to all toneless moras.

While this analysis makes the correct empirical predictions, there are two elements of it that are problematic. First, the conditioning environments for Prefix Tone Assignment and the default Lo assignment are basically the same in each case, viz., a toneless TBU. What would motivate a toneless TBU to be realized with a Hi tone at one stage of the derivation, and with a Lo tone at another? A second (more serious) problem concerns the role of the Obligatory Contour Principle (OCP). Casali invokes the OCP in order to explain why Prefix Tone Assignment does not assign a Hi tone to the prefix when there is already a Hi tone in the stem. However, when a Lo tone is assigned by default to all toneless moras, both the prefix and the first TBU of the stem are assigned the same Lo tone. To be consistent, Prefix Tone Assignment should assign to the prefix a Hi tone which then merges with the Hi of the stem.

Two final rules of relevance to the data in (74) are Lexical *h*-Spread (LHS), formalized in (78), and Final *l*-Docking (FLD), formalized in (79).

(78)   Lexical *h*-Spread

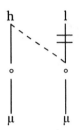

(79)   Final *l*-Docking (postlexical)

LHS is a lexical rule that applies after *l*-Assignment. When an associated *h* is followed by an associated *l*, the *h* spreads rightwards to the TRN of the *l* and delinks the *l*. Because the target of the spreading is the TRN, the spreading affects all of the TBUs that are linked to the TRN. Notice that there is no need to refer to *Hs* and *Ls* in this rule because they are not yet present at this stage of the derivation. So *h* suffices, in essence, to spread both sets of features. FLD is a postlexical rule that reassociates a final floating *l* to the final TRN of the utterance, thereby creating a Hi-falling contour. This is demonstrated in (80).

(80)   Underlying Form   *í-jono*

        h-Deletion   -

        l-Assignment   *í-jònò*

        h-Spread   *í-jónó`*

        FLD (postlexical)   *íjónô*

        Surface Form   [íjónô]   'dogs'

Lexical and postlexical derivations for each of the forms in (74) appear in appendices A and B, respectively, at the end of the chapter.

4.2 Associative construction

We now look at tonal alternations in the associative (noun-noun) construction. In this construction, which translates as "X's Y" (discussed later), one can juxtapose almost any noun with any noun. When juxtaposed, the six surface melodies represented in (74) combine to yield the thirty-six forms in (81). Forms to the left of the arrows represent the output of the lexical level. Lexical and postlexical derivations for each of the forms in (81) appear in appendices A and C, respectively, at the end of the chapter.

(81)   Nouns with monomorphemic CVCV roots in noun-noun construction

1.	kìsíbɔ́	kìsíbɔ́	→	kìsíbɔ́ kíˈsíbɔ́	'ear's ear'
2.	kìbújî	kìsíbɔ́	→	kìbújí kìsíbɔ́	'grindstone's ear'
3.	kùkùtí	kìsíbɔ́	→	kùkùtí kíˈsíbɔ́	'orange's ear'
4.	kípínî	kìsíbɔ́	→	kípíní kìsíbɔ́	'mortar's ear'
5.	naatí	kìsíbɔ́	→	naatí kíˈsíbɔ́	'cow's ear'
6.	jònò	kìsíbɔ́	→	jònò kìsíbɔ́	'dog's ear'

7.	kìsíbɔ́	kìbújî	→	kìsíbɔ́ kíˈbújî	'ear's grindstone'
8.	kìbújî	kìbújî	→	kìbújí kìbújî	'grindstone's grindstone'
9.	kùkùtí	kìbújî	→	kùkùtí kíˈbújî	'orange's grindstone'
10.	kípínî	kìbújî	→	kípíní kìbújî	'mortar's grindstone'
11.	naatí	kìbújî	→	naatí kíˈbújî	'cow's grindstone'
12.	jònò	kìbújî	→	jònò kìbújî	'dog's grindstone'

13.	kìsíbɔ́	kùkùtí	→	kìsíbɔ́ kúkùtí	'ear's orange'
14.	kìbújî	kùkùtí	→	kìbújí kùkùtí	'grindstone's orange'
15.	kùkùtí	kùkùtí	→	kùkùtí kúkùtí	'orange's orange'
16.	kípínî	kùkùtí	→	kípíní kùkùtí	'mortar's orange'
17.	naatí	kùkùtí	→	naatí kúkùtí	'cow's orange'
18.	jònò	kùkùtí	→	jònò kùkùtí	'dog's orange'

19.	kìsíbɔ́	kípíní̂	→	kìsíbɔ́ kípíní̂	'ear's mortar'
20.	kìbújî	kípíní̂	→	kìbújí ꜜkípíní̂	'grindstone's mortar'
21.	kùkùtí	kípíní̂	→	kùkùtí kípíní̂	'orange's mortar'
22.	kípíní̂	kípíní̂	→	kípíní ꜜkípíní̂	'mortar's mortar'
23.	náatí	kípíní̂	→	náatí kípíní̂	'cow's mortar'
24.	jònò	kípíní̂	→	jònò kípíní̂	'dog's mortar'
25.	kìsíbɔ́	náatí	→	kìsíbɔ́ náatí	'ear's cow'
26.	kìbújî	náatí	→	kìbújí ꜜnáatí	'grindstone's cow'
27.	kùkùtí	náatí	→	kùkùtí náatí	'orange's cow'
28.	kípíní̂	náatí	→	kípíní ꜜnáatí	'mortar's cow'
29.	náatí	náatí	→	náatí náatí	'cow's cow'
30.	jònò	náatí	→	jònò náatí	'dog's cow'
31.	kìsíbɔ́	jònò	→	kìsíbɔ́ jónò	'ear's dog'
32.	kìbújî	jònò	→	kìbújí jònò	'grindstone's dog'
33.	kùkùtí	jònò	→	kùkùtí jónò	'orange's dog'
34.	kípíní̂	jònò	→	kípíní jònò	'mortar's dog'
35.	náatí	jònò	→	náatí jónò	'cow's dog'
36.	jònò	jònò	→	jònò jònò	'dog's dog'

In the following discussion I first argue that there is no "associative" morpheme between the nouns in the Chumburung associative construction, and then I account for the tonal alternations in (81).

In a typical associative construction, a possessive that means 'cat's claw' has the word order *claw cat*, with an associative morpheme between the nouns that translates roughly as 'of'. The associative construction in Chumburung, however, is quite different from this. In Chumburung the meaning 'cat's claw' has the order *cat claw*, which is opposite to that of the typical associative construction. From the examples in (81) it is obvious that there is no segmental morpheme between the nouns in this construction. Less clear, of course, is whether there is a morpheme consisting of a floating tone. None of the examples in (81), however, suggests a floating tone hypothesis, and indeed many of them would be difficult to explain if there were floating tones involved. The examples in (82), taken from (81), are illustrative.

`(82)   a. *jònò jònò*   → *jònò jònò* 'dog's dog' (#36, (81))

          b. *náatí náatí*   → *náatí náatí* 'cow's cow' (#29, (81))

The nouns in (82a) are each pronounced Lo in isolation. The fact that they exhibit no tonal alternation when juxtaposed suggests that there is no non-Lo floating tone involved in the construction. Similarly, the lack of alternation in (82b) suggests that there is no non-Hi floating tone involved in the construction.

The tonal alternations in (81) are accounted for in a relatively straightforward manner. Within phonological phrases in Chumburung, a word-final Hi spreads rightwards across a word boundary to the first TBU of a second word and delinks the Lo from that TBU. Postlexical Hi-Spread (PHS) is formalized in (83).

(83)   Postlexical Hi-Spread

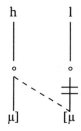

PHS spreads a word-final Hi tone from the TRN rightwards across a word boundary to the first TBU of the following word, provided that the TBU is Lo-toned. The Lo is subsequently delinked from that TBU.[27] Compare examples (84a, b) with (84c).

(84)   a. *náatí kùkùtí*   → *náatí kúkùtí* 'cow's orange' (# 17, (81))

          b. *náatí jònò*   → *náatí jónò* 'cow's dog' (# 35, (81))

          c. *kípíní jònò*   → *kípíní jònò* 'mortar's dog' (# 34, (81))

---

[27]An alternative formalism of PHS would spread the *h* to the TRN of the *l*, as in the lexical version of the rule. This would involve stipulating that the target of the spreading was the TBU, and would result in splitting the node of an *l* that was multiply linked (cf. the discussion in chapter 3 on node fission). Such a formalism would correctly spread the *h*, however, as a postlexical rule it would apply simultaneously with Postlexical Default Feature Assignment (discussed next). Postlexical Default Feature Assignment would incorrectly assign the tonal feature *L* to this (target) TRN because the TRN would be linked to an *l* in the input to both rules.

In (84a), the second word begins with a Lo-toned prefix, and in (84b), the second word does not begin with a prefix; in both cases, the final Hi tone of the first word spreads to the first TBU of the second word. In (84c), even though the final TBU of the first word is Hi-toned, the Hi itself is not final since there is a floating Lo following it. It is, therefore, not eligible to undergo spreading.

Features on the Tonal tier are not contrastive in Chumburung, and so are filled in by default in the postlexical component. Postlexical Default Feature Assignment is formalized in (85).

(85)   Postlexical Default Feature Assignment (PDFA)

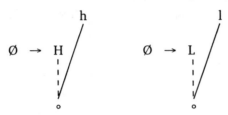

The tonal feature *H* is assigned to TRNs already associated to *h*, and the tonal feature *L* to TRNs already associated to *l* (cf. the reference to Enhancement Theory in chapter 2).

4.3 Automatic downstep

In Chumburung, whenever a Hi tone follows a Lo tone within a phonological phrase, there is automatic downstep; i.e., the Hi is realized on the same (lower) register as the Lo. Following common practice, the phonetic effect of automatic downstep is not indicated in the examples in (81). Automatic downstep is accounted for by the rule of *l*-Spread in (86).

(86)   *l*-Spread (postlexical)

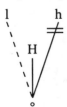

l-Spread is a postlexical rule that spreads a register feature *l* (either associated or floating) to the TRN to its right and dissociates the *h* from that node. Because the target of the spreading is the TRN, the spreading affects all of the TBUs that are linked to the TRN. *l*-Spread applies after Postlexical Default Feature Assignment (ensured by the presence of the tonal feature *H* in the formalism). If it were to apply before default assignment of the tonal features, the default rules would (incorrectly) insert *L* on these TRNs.

  PDFA and *l*-Spread are demonstrated in this next example, taken from #13, (81).

(87)   Output of lexical component   PDFA

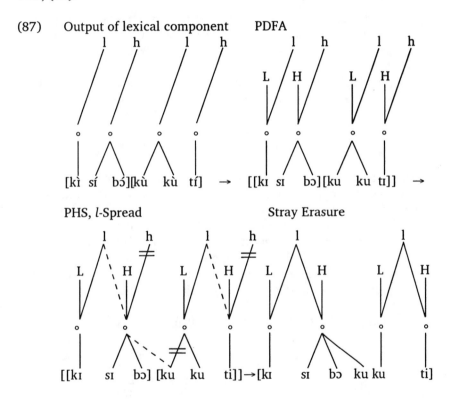

PHS, *l*-Spread   Stray Erasure

Phonetic representation

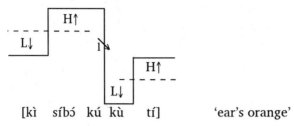

[kì síbɔ́ kú kù   tí]   'ear's orange'

In (87) PHS applies with the result that the first Lo-toned *kù* is phoneti-cally realized at the same pitch as the preceding Hi-toned *síbɔ́*. *l*-Spread also applies so that the pitch of all Hi-toned TBUs is realized on the same register as the Lo tone that precedes them. Notice that the level of the Lo tone on the first register is phonetically the same as the Hi on the following lower regis-ter. This is because the register/tone ratio in Chumburung is 1/1.

4.4 Nonautomatic downstep

We next look at nonautomatic downstep in Chumburung. As stated else-where, the difference between automatic downstep and nonautomatic downstep is that for nonautomatic downstep, the Lo tone that is responsi-ble for it is not phonetically realized. Nonautomatic downstep derives from three sources in Chumburung. The first is the Postlexical Hi-Spread rule formalized in (83). Whenever application of PHS results in a floating Lo between Hi's, downstep occurs. The structural descriptions of both PHS and *l*-Spread are met in (88), from #5 in (81).

(88)   Output of lexical component   PDFA

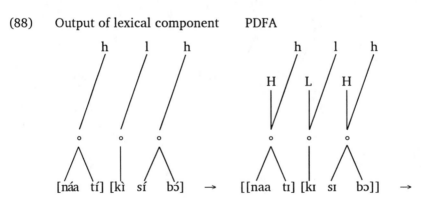

PHS, *l*-Spread   Stray Erasure

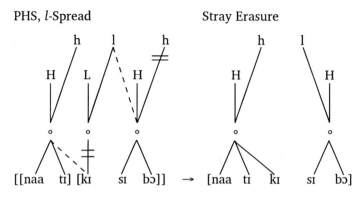

Phonetic representation

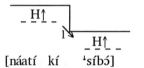

[náatí kí   ꜜsíbɔ́]   'cow's ear'

In this example, PHS applies, represented by the leftmost dotted association line, and the Lo is set floating. The first three TBUs of the utterance are, therefore, pronounced at the same (high) pitch level. In addition, the register *l* spreads rightwards onto the TRN above *sibɔ* represented by the rightmost dotted line. Since *sibɔ* is now associated to the register *l*, the register is lowered (downstepped) with respect to the preceding TBU (viz., *kı*).

The second source of nonautomatic downstep in Chumburung derives from the rule of Lexical *h*-Spread. We see this in examples like (89), from #28 in (81).

(89)   Underlying form   *l*-Assignment, Merger

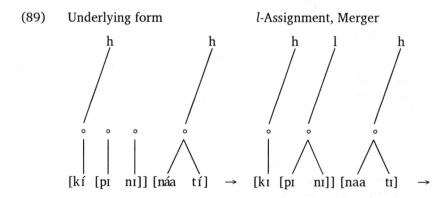

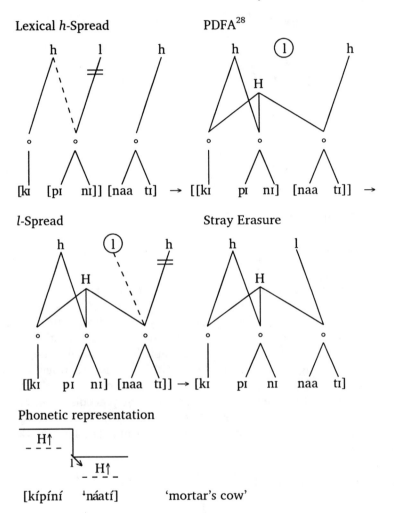

Phonetic representation

[kípíní ꜛnáatí]   'mortar's cow'

The third source of nonautomatic downstep in Chumburung derives from words that end in a glottal stop utterance finally. Snider (1986) shows that many words that end in a glottal stop utterance finally have also

---

[28] I assume that in languages for which the OCP is a valid constraint when adjacent TRNs meet the structural description of the same default feature assignment rule, they are assigned the *same* default feature. Since the TRNs in this example are adjacent and meet the structural description for PDFA, they are linked to a single *H*.

undergone apocope (i.e., lost a final segment, or segments) historically.[29] As a result, those words that have undergone apocope and end in a Hi tone in isolation are tonally indistinguishable from "normal" words that also end in a Hi tone in isolation. However, in the context of a following Hi tone, many of the words that have undergone apocope cause the following Hi tone to be downstepped.[30]

(90)   a. dá ꜜnáátí 'older brother's cow' *(cf. dáʔ* 'older brother' and *náátí* 'cow')
         b. dàáʔ 'older brother' (Nawuri), dâáʔ 'older brother' (Gichode)

In (90a), *dáʔ* ends in a glottal stop utterance finally. When followed by the word *náátí* 'cow', the glottal stop is deleted, and the Hi tone of *náátí* is downstepped. The fact that downstep occurs suggests that there is a Lo tone involved, a suggestion supported by the Nawuri and Gichode words in (90b) that are cognate with *dáʔ*. In Nawuri and Gichode, which are closely related to Chumburung, both cognate words are realized with Hi-falling tones on long vowels. That the Lo tone is part of *dáʔ* and not *náátí* can be further deduced from the failure of *náátí* to undergo downstep in contexts like (82b), when it follows other words that end in Hi tone but which have not undergone apocope.

A first possible analysis of words like *dáʔ* is that they are simply words that end in a floating Lo tone underlyingly. Recall however, that in Chumburung Lo tones are unspecified in underlying forms. (This could leave one in the awkward position of positing unspecified, i.e., toneless, floating tones!) I propose that the glottal stop in words like *dáʔ* belongs to a degenerate (i.e., nonsonorant) TBU, a vestige perhaps of a former sonorant TBU. This TBU continues to dominate a TRN, which in the case of words like *dáʔ* is underlyingly toneless. Follow the derivation in (91).

---

[29]Since noun roots appear historically to have been limited to two or fewer syllables, utterance final glottal stops are found only on monomorphemic monosyllabic stems or on compound stems whose final morpheme is monosyllabic. For this reason, words that end in glottal stop are not found in (74) and (81).

[30]Although many of the words that end in Hi tone and glottal stop utterance finally cause a following Hi tone to be downstepped, not all do. For example, ɔ̀tʃí náátí 'woman's cow' (cf. ɔ̀tʃíʔ 'woman'). For words like ɔ̀tʃíʔ, I assume that the TBU that was lost histori- cally was Hi-toned.

(91)   Underlying form   *l*-Assignment   *h*-Spread   Merger

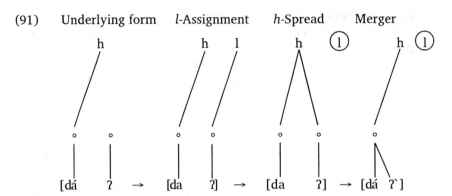

In this derivation, the glottal stop dominates an underlyingly toneless TRN. A Lo tone is assigned by default and is then delinked as a result of Lexical *h*-Spread.

Example (92) shows the postlexical derivation of *dá ⁺nǎǎtí* (from (90)).

(92)   Output of lexical component (cf. (91))

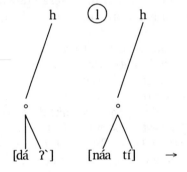

PDFA, Glottal Del., *l*-Spread

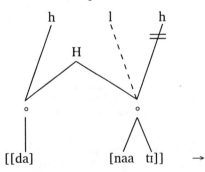

Stray Erasure   Phonetic representation

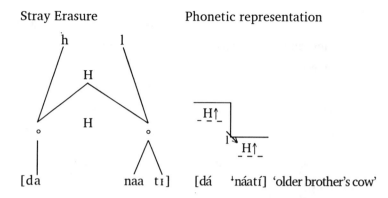

[da   naa tɪ]   [dá   ꜛnáatí] 'older brother's cow'

In (92) the glottal stop is deleted utterance medially and the floating register *l* spreads rightwards onto the TRN of *nǎǎtí*. This spreading delinks the
register *h* and lowers the tonal register.

This concludes the study of downstep in Chumburung. The foregoing
discussions describe the six surface tonal melodies found on
monomorphemic CVCV noun stems in Chumburung and provide an analysis of how they are derived both lexically and postlexically. They also describe and account for the surface patterns that emerge when each melody
is juxtaposed with itself and with each other melody. Instances of
downstep are prevalent throughout the data, and in each case can be said
to occur when the second of two adjacent TBUs is associated to an *l* that is
not also associated to the preceding TBU.

Appendix A: Lexical derivations of forms in (74)

The output of these derivations is used as input to the forms in (80), as
well as input to the forms in appendix B and appendix C.

	'cow'	'cows'	'fetish'	'fetishes'
Underlying Form	*náatí*	*í-náatí*	*kísi*	*í-kísi*
h-Deletion	—	*ɪ-náatí*	—	*i-kísi*
l-Assignment	—	*ì-náatí*	*kísì*	*ì-kísì*
Lexical *h*-Spread	—	—	*kísí`*	*ì-kísí`*
Output of Lex.	*náatí*	*ì-náatí*	*kísí`*	*ìkísí`*

	'goat'	'goats'	'dog'	'dogs'
Underlying Form	tɪrí	í-tɪrí	jono	í-jono
h-Deletion	—	ɪ-tɪrí	—	—
l-Assignment	tìrí	ì-tìrí	jònò	í-jònò
Lexical h-Spread	—	—	—	í-jónó `
Output of Lex.	tìrí	ìtìrí	jònò	íjónó `

	'ear'	'ears'	'grindstone'	'grindstones'
Underlying Form	kí-síbɔ́	á-síbɔ́	kí-bújɪ	ɔ́-bújɪ
h-Deletion	kɪ-síbɔ́	a-síbɔ́	kɪ-bújɪ	ɔ-bújɪ
l-Assignment	kì-síbɔ́	à-síbɔ́	kì-bújì	ɔ̀-bújì
Lexical h-Spread	—	—	kì-bújí `	ɔ̀-bújí `
Output of Lex.	kì-síbɔ́	àsíbɔ́	kìbújí `	ɔ̀bújí `

	'orange'	'oranges'	'mortar'	'mortars'
Underlying Form	kú-kutí	ɔ́-kutí	kí-pɪrʊ	á-pɪrʊ
h-Deletion	ku-kutí	ɔ-kutí	—	—
l-Assignment	kù-kùtí	ɔ̀-kùtí	kí-pìnì	á-pìnì
Lexical h-Spread	—	—	kí-píní `	á-píní `
Output of Lex.	kùkùtí	ɔ̀kùtí	kípíní `	ápíní `

The output of these derivations is not the Surface Form, as might perhaps be expected, but rather the output of the lexical component. Since the
rule of Final l-Docking is postlexical, its application is not included in these
derivations. One potential question that arises is why h-Deletion does not
delete the first h of forms like *náatí* 'cow'. The answer is that forms like *náatí*
consist of a monomorphemic stem with only one h that is underlyingly associated to both TBUs. h-Deletion can only apply when there are two underlying hs.

Appendix B: Postlexical derivations of forms in (74)

	'cow'	'cows'	'fetish'	'fetishes'
Output of Lex.	náatí	ìnáatí	kísí `	ìkísí `
Post Lex. Hi-Spr.	—	—	—	—
l-Spread	—	not shown	—	not shown
Final l-Docking	—	—	kísî	ìkísî
Surface Form	[náatí]	[ìnáatí]	[kísî]	[ìkísî]

	'goat'	'goats'	'dog'	'dogs'
Output of Lex.	tììrí	ìtììrí	jònò	íjónó `
Post Lex. Hi-Spr.	—	—	—	—
l-Spread	not shown	not shown	—	—
Final l-Docking	—	—	—	íjónô
Surface Form	[tììrí]	[ìtììrí]	[jònò]	[íjónô]

	'ear'	'ears'	'grindstone'	'grindstones'
Output of Lex.	kìsíbɔ́	àsíbɔ́	kìbújí `	ɔ̀bújí `
Post Lex. Hi-Spr.	—	—	—	—
l-Spread	not shown	not shown	not shown	not shown
Final l-Docking	—	—	kìdábôŋ	àdábôŋ
Surface Form	[kìsíbɔ́]	[àsíbɔ́]	[kìdábôŋ]	[àdábôŋ]

	'orange'	'oranges'	'mortar'	'mortars'
Output of Lex.	kùkùtí	ɔ̀kùtí	kípíní `	ápíní `
Post Lex. Hi-Spr.	—	—	—	—
l-Spread	not shown	not shown	—	—
Final l-Docking	—	—	kípínî	ápínî
Surface Form	[kùkùtí]	[ɔ̀kùtí]	[kípínî]	[ápínî]

Appendix C: Postlexical derivations of forms in (81)

	1. 'ear's ear'		2. 'grindstone's ear'	
Output of Lex.	kìsíbɔ́	kìsíbɔ́	kìbújí `	kìsíbɔ́
Post Lex. Hi-Spr.	kìsíbɔ́	kí `síbɔ́	—	
l-Spread	kìsíbɔ́	kíˡsíbɔ́	not shown	
Final l-Docking	—		—	
Surface Form	[kìsíbɔ́	kíˡsíbɔ́]	[kìbújí	kìsíbɔ́]

	3. 'orange's ear'		4. 'mortar's ear'	
Output of Lex.	kùkùtí	kìsíbɔ́	kípíní `	kìsíbɔ́
Post Lex. Hi-Spr.	kùkùtí	kí `síbɔ́	—	
l-Spread	kùkùtí	kíˡsíbɔ́	not shown	
Final l-Docking	—		—	
Surface Form	[kùkùtí	kíˡsíbɔ́]	[kípíní	kìsíbɔ́]

	5. 'cow's ear'		6. 'dog's ear'	
Output of Lex.	nɗaatí	kìsíbɔ́	jònò	kìsíbɔ́
Post Lex. Hi-Spr.	nɗaatí	kí `síbɔ́	—	
l-Spread	nɗaatí	kíˡsíbɔ́	not shown	
Final l-Docking	—		—	
Surface Form	[náatí	kíˡsíbɔ́]	[jònò	kìsíbɔ́]

	7. 'ear's grindstone'		8. 'grindstone's grindstone'	
Output of Lex.	kìsíbɔ́	kìbújí `	kìbújí `	kìbújí `
Post Lex. Hi-Spr.	kìsíbɔ́	kí `bújí `	—	
l-Spread	kìsíbɔ́	kíˡbújí `	not shown	
Final l-Docking	kìsíbɔ́	kíˡbújî	kìbújí	kìbújî
Surface Form	[kìsíbɔ́	kíˡbújî]	[kìbújí	kìbújî]

	9. 'orange's grindstone'		10. 'mortar's grindstone'	
Output of Lex.	kùkùtí	kìbújí `	kípíní `	kìbújí `
Post Lex. Hi-Spr.	kùkùtí	kí `bújí `	—	
l-Spread	kùkùtí	kíˡbújí `	not shown	
Final l-Docking	kùkùtí	kíˡbújî	kípíní	kìbújî
Surface Form	[kùkùtí	kíˡbújî]	[kípíní	kìbújî]

	11. 'cow's grindstone'		12. 'dog's grindstone'	
Output of Lex.	nɗaatí	kìbújí `	jònò	kìbújí `
Post Lex. Hi-Spr.	nɗaatí	kí `bújí `	—	
l-Spread	nɗaatí	kíˡbújí `	not shown	
Final l-Docking	nɗaatí	kíˡbújî	jònò	kìbújî
Surface Form	[náatí	kíˡbújî]	[jònò	kìbújî]

	13. 'ear's orange'		14. 'grindstone's orange'	
Output of Lex.	kìsíbɔ́	kùkùtí	kìbújí `	kùkùtí
Post Lex. Hi-Spr.	kìsíbɔ́	kúkùtí	—	
l-Spread	not shown		not shown	
Final l-Docking	—		—	
Surface Form	[kìsíbɔ́	kúkùtí]	[kìbújí	kùkùtí]

	15. 'orange's orange'		16. 'mortar's orange'	
Output of Lex.	kùkùtí	kùkùtí	kípíní `	kùkùtí
Post Lex. Hi-Spr.	kùkùtí	kúkùtí	—	
l-Spread	not shown		not shown	
Final l-Docking	—		—	
Surface Form	[kùkùtí	kúkùtí]	[kípíní	kùkùtí]

	17. 'cow's orange'		18. 'dog's orange'	
Output of Lex.	náatí	kùkùtí	jònò	kùkùtí
Post Lex. Hi-Spr.	náatí	kúkùtí	—	
l-Spread	not shown		not shown	
Final l-Docking	—		—	
Surface Form	[náatí	kúkùtí]	[jònò	kùkùtí]

	19. 'ear's mortar'		20. 'grindstone's mortar'	
Output of Lex.	kìsíbɔ́	kípíní `	kìbújí `	kípíní `
Post Lex. Hi-Spr.	—		—	
l-Spread	not shown		kìbújí	ꜛkípíní `
Final l-Docking	kìsíbɔ́	kípínî	kìbújí	ꜛkípínî
Surface Form	[kìsíbɔ́	kípínî]	[kìbújí	ꜛkípínî]

	21. 'orange's mortar'		22. 'mortar's mortar'	
Output of Lex.	kùkùtí	kípíní `	kípíní `	kípíní `
Post Lex. Hi-Spr.	—		—	
l-Spread	not shown		kípíní	ꜛkípíní `
Final l-Docking	kùkùtí	kípínî	kípíní	ꜛkípínî
Surface Form	[kùkùtí	kípínî]	[kípíní	ꜛkípínî]

	23. 'cow's mortar'		24. 'dog's mortar'	
Output of Lex.	náatí	kípíní `	jònò	kípíní `
Post Lex. Hi-Spr.	—		—	
l-Spread	—		not shown	
Final l-Docking	náatí	kípínî	jònò	kípínî
Surface Form	[náatí	kípínî]	[jònò	kípínî]

The Geometry and Features of Tone

25. 'ear's cow'

Output of Lex.	kìsíbɔ́	náatí
Post Lex. Hi-Spr.	—	
l-Spread	not shown	
Final l-Docking	—	
Surface Form	[kìsíbɔ́	náatí]

26. 'grindstone's cow'

Output of Lex.	kìbújí `	náatí
Post Lex. Hi-Spr.	—	
l-Spread	kìbújí	ꜜnáatí
Final l-Docking	—	
Surface Form	[kìbújí	ꜜnáatí]

27. 'orange's cow'

Output of Lex.	kùkùtí	náatí
Post Lex. Hi-Spr.	—	
l-Spread	not shown	
Final l-Docking	—	
Surface Form	[kùkùtí	náatí]

28. 'mortar's cow'

Output of Lex.	kípíní `	náatí
Post Lex. Hi-Spr.	—	
l-Spread	kípíní	ꜜnáatí
Final l-Docking	—	
Surface Form	[kípíní	ꜜnáatí]

29. 'cow's cow'

Output of Lex.	náatí	náatí
Post Lex. Hi-Spr.	—	
l-Spread	—	
Final l-Docking	—	
Surface Form	[náatí	náatí]

30. 'dog's cow'

Output of Lex.	jònò	náatí
Post Lex. Hi-Spr.	—	
l-Spread	not shown	
Final l-Docking	—	
Surface Form	[jònò	náatí]

31. 'ear's dog'

Output of Lex.	kìsíbɔ́	jònò
Post Lex. Hi-Spr.	kìsíbɔ́	jónò
l-Spread	not shown	
Final l-Docking	—	
Surface Form	[kìsíbɔ́	jónò]

32. 'grindstone's dog'

Output of Lex.	kìbújí `	jònò
Post Lex. Hi-Spr.	—	
l-Spread	not shown	
Final l-Docking	—	
Surface Form	[kìbújí	jònò]

33. 'orange's dog'

Output of Lex.	kùkùtí	jònò
Post Lex. Hi-Spr.	kùkùtí	jónò
l-Spread	not shown	
Final l-Docking	—	
Surface Form	[kùkùtí	jónò]

34. 'mortar's dog'

Output of Lex.	kípíní `	jònò
Post Lex. Hi-Spr.	—	
l-Spread	not shown	
Final l-Docking	—	
Surface Form	[kípíní	jònò]

35. 'cow's dog'

Output of Lex.	náatí	jònò
Post Lex. Hi-Spr.	náatí	jónò
l-Spread	not shown	
Final l-Docking	—	
Surface Form	[náatí	jónò]

36. 'dog's dog'

Output of Lex.	jònò	jònò
Post Lex. Hi-Spr.	—	
l-Spread	not shown	
Final l-Docking	—	
Surface Form	[jònò	jònò]

5
Nonterracing Downstep in Engenni

5.1 Introduction

Although Thomas (1974, 1978) describes Engenni, a Kwa language spoken in Nigeria, as having three levels of surface pitch with restrictions on the top and middle levels, she analyzes the system as having only two contrasting tonemes, Lo and Hi. In addition, there is what she calls "automatic upstep."[31]

As discussed earlier, upstep can be described as the phonological shifting upwards of the tonal register within a phonological phrase, similar in nature to changing to a higher key in a score of music. Upstep in Engenni is predictable and results in the shifting upwards of a Hi tone whenever a Lo tone follows the Hi. Examples of this appear in (93) and (94).[32]

---

[31]This chapter is an adaptation of Snider (to appear) and appears here with permission from *The Journal of West African Languages*.

[32]Most of the data in this chapter are taken from Thomas (1974, 1978). Although I have included all glosses as they are provided in the source documents, I have taken the liberty to replace certain of Thomas' phonetic symbols with their IPA equivalents. In some cases, more detail would have been desirable, but this information was not available to me. I have similarly accepted Thomas' underlying forms as provided. Although I have no reason to question their validity, at the same time I would have preferred to have been able to include more evidence to support them.

(93)   a.   b.

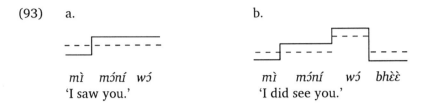

mì   mɔ́nɪ́ wɔ́   mì   mɔ́nɪ́ wɔ́ bhɛ̀ɛ̀
'I saw you.'   'I did see you.'

In (93a) wɔ́ is realized at the same level as the Hi-toned tone-bearing units (TBUs) that precede it. This may be contrasted with (93b) in which a Lo tone follows wɔ́. In this case, the Hi tone of wɔ́ is upstepped relative to the Hi-toned TBUs that precede it.

(94)   a.   b.

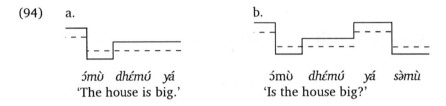

ɔ́mʊ̀ dhɛ́mʊ́ yá   ɔ́mʊ̀ dhɛ́mʊ́ yá sɑ̀mʊ̀
'The house is big.'   'Is the house big?'

Example (94) is similar to (93) except that the utterance begins with Hi tone. Again, each time a Hi-toned TBU tone precedes a Lo-toned TBU, the Hi-toned TBU is upstepped relative to preceding Hi-toned TBUs. So far, the data that support the claims made to this point would also be consistent with another possible analysis in which there are three underlying tones, Hi, Mid, and Lo, and a rule that lowers Hi tones to Mid in utterance-final position. Looking again at (93) and (94), the data support this in that wɔ́ and yá are Hi utterance medially, and Mid utterance finally. This possible analysis can be ruled out, however, by looking at the data in (95).

(95)   a.   b.

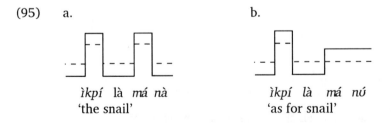

ìkpí là má nà   ìkpí là má nʊ́
'the snail'   'as for snail'

In (95a), although má is phonetically realized as Hi utterance medially before a Lo tone, it is realized as Mid *also utterance medially* in (95b) when it is followed by a Hi tone. This shows that Hi is not lowered to Mid in utterance-final position, and further supports the claim that a Hi tone in Engenni is upstepped relative to preceding Hi's only when the Hi is followed by a Lo tone. Another example appears in (96) in which the utterance begins with a Hi-toned TBU, but in this case it is not immediately followed by a Lo tone.

(96)

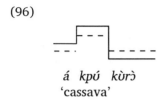

á kpú kùrɔ̀
'cassava'

As can be seen in (96), it is only when a Hi-toned TBU occurs immediately before a Lo tone that it is upstepped.

Upstep also occurs when the tone-bearing support for the Lo tone is deleted. "When two vowels come together at a word boundary, the first vowel together with its tone is elided" (Thomas 1974:14, 15). This may be seen in (97).

(97)   a.

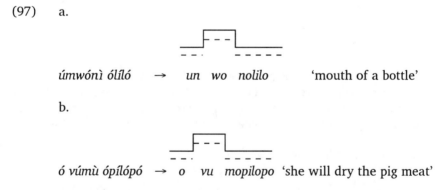

úmwónì ólíló   →   un wo nolilo   'mouth of a bottle'

b.

ó vúmù ópílópó   →   o   vu mopilopo 'she will dry the pig meat'

In these examples, even though the tone-bearing support of the Lo tone in each case has been elided, upstep on the immediately preceding Hi still occurs.

One way to analyze this is to simply say, as Thomas does, that a Hi tone before a Lo tone is "upstepped," or raised. But there is no real motivation for this raising. The examples in (94) shed additional light on the subject. An alternative way to analyze this phenomenon is to consider that in (94a) the Lo-toned mù and everything to its right is downstepped relative to the preceding Hi-toned ɔ́. In this respect it behaves just like normal downstepping languages. When Lo-toned sɔ̀mù is added to this sentence, as in (94b), the downstep effect stops short one TBU before the Lo tone. This leaves the Hi-toned *yá* non-downstepped relative to the preceding downstepped Hi tone.[33]

5.2 Analysis

By analyzing Engenni tone as a nonterracing downstep system, and by couching this analysis within the RTT framework, the Engenni tone system can be described in a manner that is only minimally different from other downstep systems.

In Engenni, as in many West African languages, a Hi tone that follows a Lo tone is always lower than a Hi tone that precedes the Lo tone, but higher than the Lo tone itself. This is typically called downdrift or automatic downstep, and a clear example of it appears in (98), repeated from (94a).

(98)

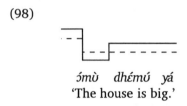

ɔ́mù   dhɛ́mú   yá
'The house is big.'

When automatic downstep occurs, the Hi tone that follows the Lo tone assimilates to the lower register of the Lo tone, and is consequently realized on a register that is lower than any Hi tone that precedes the Lo tone. We can account for this phenomenon with the *l*-Spread rule of (99).

(99)   *l*-Spread (postlexical and iterative)

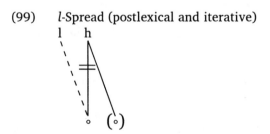

In (7), an *l*, whether floating or associated, spreads rightwards and delinks a following *h* from its TRN, subject to the following condition. If there is another TRN following the first TRN, the second TRN must also be

---

[33]Thomas (1974) considers, but rejects, an analysis similar to this on grounds that her analysis is simpler. In the conclusion, I will argue that the present proposal is more explanatory.

associated to the *h* register feature. This is because there is a constraint in Engenni against a floating *h* register feature occurring between associated *l* register features. Stated another way, the constraint prevents two *l* register features from being associated to adjacent TRNs.

A tentative derivation of (98) appears in (100). For each of the derivations in the remainder of this chapter, the input is fully specified and assumes the prior filling in of any and all default features.

(100)   Input   *l*-Spread

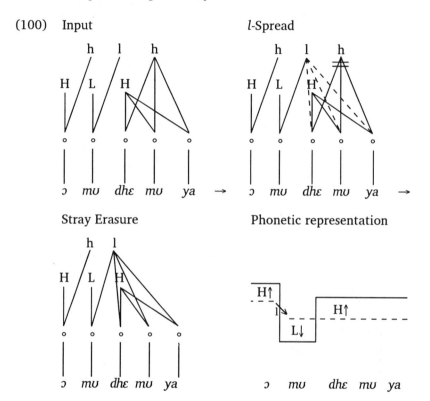

In (100), application of *l*-Spread spreads the register *l* to all of the TRNs to its right, delinking the register *h*s. Subsequently, a rule of Stray Erasure deletes all unassociated (i.e., floating) elements.

Although the rule of *l*-Spread in (99) accounts for the examples in (93) and (94) in a straightforward manner, in order to account for examples like (96), it is further necessary to assume that Engenni assigns by default a floating *l* register boundary tone to the left edge of phonological phrases. This is stated in (101).

(101)   Phrasal Boundary Tone Assignment

       Assign a floating *l* to the left edge of the phonological phrase.

   We now show derivations for some of the examples above. Notice that in (102) and (103), the application of Phrasal Boundary Tone Assignment does not have any effect on the surface realization. This is because in both cases, the boundary *l* is followed immediately by a lexical *l* with which it merges, due to OCP constraints. In (104), however, Phrasal Boundary Tone Assignment does make a difference.

(102)   Input   Phrasal Boundary Tone Assignment

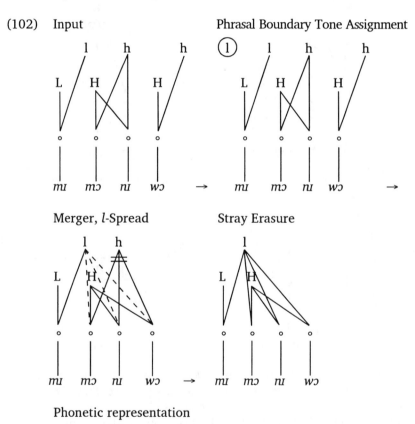

       Phonetic representation

                    'I saw you.'

In (102), taken from (93a), Phrasal Boundary Tone Assignment inserts a floating register *l* at the left edge of the utterance. Next, Merger coalesces identical adjacent features, and the rule of *l*-Spread spreads the register *l* to all of the TRNs to its right, delinking the register *hs*. Finally, Stray Erasure deletes all unassociated elements. For this example, the application or nonapplication of Phrasal Boundary Tone Assignment is irrelevant because the register *l* that is assigned by this rule is merged with the initial *l* of the phrase through application of Merger. Since all TBUs are now associated to the same register feature, the Hi and Lo tones of the utterance are both realized on the same register, as indicated in the phonetic representation for (102).

We next look at an example in which *l*-Spread does not delink all of the *h* register features.

(103)   Input   Phrasal Boundary Tone Assignment

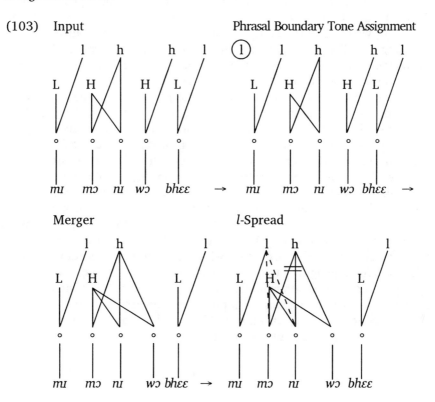

Phonetic representation

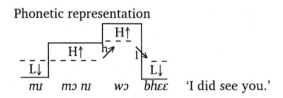

mɪ   mɔ nɪ   wɔ   bhɛɛ   'I did see you.'

In (103), taken from (93b), Phrasal Boundary Tone Assignment assigns a floating register *l* to the left edge of the utterance, and, similar to (102), application of Merger negates any effect the application of this rule might otherwise have. Application of *l*-Spread results in the leftmost register *l* spreading rightwards and delinking the register *h* as far as the TBU *ní*. At this point, the constraint against a floating *h* register feature occurring between associated *l* register features prevents the *l* from spreading and delinking the *h* from the TRN of *wɔ́*. Interpreting the phonetic representation for (103), we see that the Lo and Hi tones of *mì mɔ́ ní* are realized on the same register. The Hi tone of *wɔ́* is realized on the next register higher, and the Lo tone of *bhɛ̀ɛ̀* is realized on the next register lower than that of *wɔ́*, that is, the same register that *mì mɔ́ ní* are realized on.

One question concerns whether or not the TBU *wɔ́* should be considered to be upstepped. Certainly *wɔ́* is upstepped relative to the preceding TBU. In the overall scheme of things, if one considers the Hi-toned TBU that precedes *wɔ́ not* to be downstepped, then one probably *should* consider *wɔ́* as being upstepped (Option A). On the other hand, if one considers the Hi-toned TBU that precedes *wɔ́* to be downstepped (present analysis), then one probably should consider *wɔ́* as being non-downstepped (Option B). Choosing between these two options is not as arbitrary as it might first appear to be. In the case of Option B (downstep/non-downstep), the downstep is motivated in that the Hi tones that undergo the downstep are preceded by Lo tones, an environment which is known to cause downstep in other tonal languages. But in the case of Option A (non-downstep/ upstep), there is no obvious motivation for the upstep. So I conclude that the super-Hi tone in Engenni is simply a non-downstepped Hi.

Turning now to (104), taken from (96), we have a case where Phrasal Boundary Tone Assignment does make a difference.

(104)   Input   Phrasal Boundary Tone Assignment

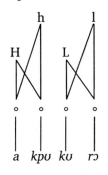

→

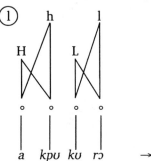

→

l-Spread   Phonetic representation

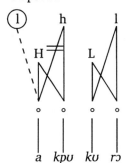

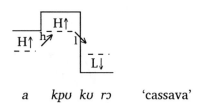

In (104), the leftmost register *l* undergoes *l*-Spread, and the spreading stops one TBU short of delinking the *h* from the TRN of *kpú*. Notice that if Phrasal Boundary Tone Assignment did not apply, there would be no register *l* to undergo *l*-Spread. The phonetic representation for (104) is interpreted similarly to that of (103).

In the examples so far, Phrasal Boundary Tone Assignment is needed in order to account for cases like (104), in which the phonological phrase begins with Hi tone and there is, superficially, a super-Hi tone in the phonetic representation. When the phrase begins with Lo tone, as in (102) and (103), whether Phrasal Boundary Tone Assignment applies or not is irrelevant since Merger coalesces the *l* it assigns with that of the initial Lo tone. The question arises whether inclusion of Phrasal Boundary Tone Assignment makes the wrong prediction for examples like (98), which do not have a super-Hi tone but which do begin with Hi tone. Recall that the tentative derivation of (98) that appears in (100) makes no reference to Phrasal Boundary Tone Assignment. A definitive derivation of (98) appears in (105). In (105), which does assume the application of Phrasal

Boundary Tone Assignment, the reader can see that application of Phrasal Boundary Tone Assignment does not result in a wrong prediction.

(105)   Input   Phrasal Boundary Tone Assignment

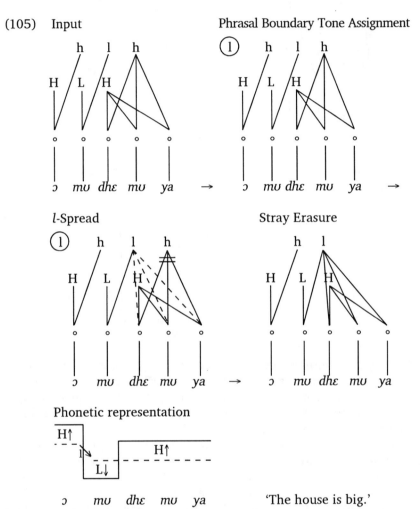

Phonetic representation

'The house is big.'

In (105), application of Phrasal Boundary Tone Assignment assigns a register *l* to the left edge of the utterance. Since spreading of that *l* would violate the constraint against two *l* register features being associated to adjacent TRNs, the application of *l*-Spread is blocked, and the (still) unassociated *l* is later deleted by Stray Erasure. The net result of (105) is therefore identical to that of (100).

5.3 Conclusion

Thomas (1974:25) considers, but rejects, an analysis very similar to the present proposal. The analysis she considers can be summarized as follows: (a) a sequence of Hi's is lowered after Lo or floating Lo, (b) a downstepped Hi reverts to the pitch of the previous Hi in the utterance before Lo, and (c) all utterance-initial Hi's are lowered. She rejects this analysis on the grounds that an analysis that simply upsteps a Hi-toned TBU before a Lo tone (one component) is simpler than one that requires the three components just stated. I deal with each of these components in the order (b), (c), and (a).

Component (b) represents a real difference between the present proposal and the analysis Thomas rejects. In her rejected analysis, the highest pitch level first undergoes lowering, and later raising. In the present proposal, it undergoes neither. This makes the present proposal one component simpler than the one she rejects.

Component (c) does pose an added complication to the present analysis. In order to account for the lowering of initial Hi tones, I suggest that languages assign by default floating Lo boundary tones to the left and right edges of utterances. In the case of Engenni, it is the left Lo boundary tone that is responsible for the lowering of initial Hi tones. Although the boundary tone proposal does add to the complexity of the analysis, its explanatory power goes beyond accounting for Engenni. By recognizing it, a number of seemingly disparate register phenomena in a broad cross-section of (at least) Niger-Congo languages can be treated in a unified manner (cf. the discussion in chapter 3).

Component (a) of Thomas' rejected analysis (i.e., a sequence of Hi's is lowered after Lo or floating Lo) is much more natural and explanatory than the analysis that Hi-toned TBUs are upstepped before Lo tones. Cross-linguistically, this component is needed anyway in order to account for downstep in many African languages.

In conclusion, the success of Register Tier Theory in accounting for the super-Hi tone of Engenni suggests that it would also prove successful in accounting for the super-Hi tones of many other African languages. Although clear cases do exist of terracing upstepped Hi tones (e.g., Acatlán Mixtec, described in Pike and Wistrand (1974) and in the following chapter, and Kimatuumbi, described in Odden (1996)), it has been a mystery why the upstep of what has often appeared to be an upstep system in many African languages affects only one TBU, and is never cumulative, i.e., it never results in upwards terracing. The emerging answer is that the super-Hi tone of these systems is not an upstepped Hi, as such, but rather a non-downstepped Hi.

6
Upstepped Hi in Acatlán Mixtec

6.1 Introduction

The Acatlán dialect of Mixtec (data from Pike and Wistrand 1974) is spoken in Mexico and has three contrastive tones, Hi, Mid, and Lo, which Pike and Wistrand label "H," "M," and "L." The contrastive nature of these tones may be seen in the minimal contrast sets in (106).

(106) a. dò?ò 'basket'   kǎā̀ 'will be perforated'   kʷà?à 'many'

        dò?ō 'mud brick' kǎā̄ 'will be accustomed to' kʷà?ā 'will give'

        dò?ó 'suffers'   kǎā́ 'perforates'   kʷà?á 'red'

        dō?ó 'we incl.'   káā̄ 'will perforate'   kʷá?ā 'makes'

        dó?ò 'tail'   káā̀ 'is perforated'   kʷá?à 'holds'

   b. yò?ò 'will twist' ?ìǐ 'salt'   tùí 'stings'

        yō?ò 'rope'   ?ǐī 'skin'   tùī 'will appear'

        yó?ò 'twists'   ?īī 'hail'   tūī 'will sting'

        yò?ó 'this'   ?ìí 'stands'   túī 'appears'

In addition to Hi, Mid, and Lo, there is a fourth tone that Pike and Wistrand call "step-up," or "U," and which occurs only following Hi or another U. "A sequence of step-up tones is a sequence of successively higher tones. A high tone which follows the step-up tone is level with it, but higher than a high which precedes the step-up tone" (Pike and Wistrand 1974:81, 82).

Upstep in Acatlán Mixtec mirrors downstep in other languages. As may be seen in the following example, the upstepped level in Acatlán Mixtec can involve more than one TBU, and terracing is possible. Unless otherwise indicated, all examples in this section follow the format of Pike and Wistrand in that the tones to the left of the arrows represent the surface pitch of each word as it is spoken in isolation.

(107)   [kàná]   [māngū] [nà?nú]   [kù?ú]   [tū]   [yùká] →
        coming^forth   mango large-P   being^seen   HAB   there

$$\overline{}$$
$$\overline{} \; \overline{} \; \overline{}$$
$$\overline{} \; \overline{}$$
$$\overline{} \; \overline{} \; \overline{} \; \overline{}$$

[kā ná mán gú ná? ˈnú kú ˈ?ú tú yú ˈká]
'The large mangos usually seen there are starting to grow.'

Setting aside (for the moment) questions concerning the cause of upstep in Acatlán Mixtec, the single intonational phrase in (107) shows that the domain of upstep is not restricted to one TBU, and that successive, terraced upsteps are allowed.

6.2 Tone classes

In their analysis, Pike and Wistrand classify any given word[34] as belonging to one of three tonal classes: Class A, Class B, or Class C. Which class a word is assigned to depends upon how it influences or does not influence the tones of words that follow it. The tone system of Acatlán Mixtec is complex, and a presentation of all the facts is beyond the scope of this study. This study is therefore confined to words of Class A and Class C.

Class A words are the most numerous, and can be considered to be "basic." When pronounced in islolation, disyllabic words of this class occur with the six surface melodies of (108).

---

[34]Although Pike and Wistrand refer to the forms in their work as "morphemes," glosses for many forms (e.g., *kīʔī* 'will be sick' and *dáˈté* 'is being shorn') suggest something of a more composite nature. For this reason, I am substituting the term "word" for their "morpheme."

(108)   [kù?ì]   'woman's sister'

        [vǎ?ná]   'sleepiness'

        [ɲū?ū]   'fire'

        [bēlú]   'hat'

        [tó?ò]   'stranger'

        [dá'té]   'is being shorn'

A cursory look at these examples shows that there is a three-way contrast (Lo, Mid, or Hi) with respect to the first tone of the melodies. I analyze these three tones as in (109).

(109)   a. Lo (toneless)   b. Mid   c. Hi

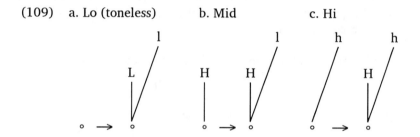

The Lo tone is underlyingly unspecified, the Mid tone is underlyingly specified for *H* tone only, and the Hi tone is underlyingly specified for *h* register only.

As can be seen in (109), all TRNs in Acatlán Mixtec are underlyingly either specified for *h* register or they are unspecified for register. If they are unspecified for register, they are assigned *l* by default in the postlexical component, regardless of any specification that might exist on the Tonal tier. Justification for the underspecification of *l* (as opposed to *h*) and for the postlexical (as opposed to lexical) default assignment of *l* is provided below. The postlexical default assignment of register *l* is formalized in (110).

(110)   Postlexical default assignment of register *l*

$\emptyset \rightarrow l$

All TRNs in Acatlán Mixtec are also underlyingly either specified for *H*
tone or they are unspecified for tone. If they are unspecified for tone they
are assigned *L* if the TRN is linked to *l* register, and *H* if the TRN is linked to
h register, in keeping with the Enhancement Theory referred to in chapter
2. This is formalized in (111).

(111)   Postlexical default assignment of tonal features

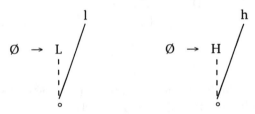

Given the assumptions in (109) regarding how the three tones are
underspecified, the six surface melodies of (108) can be accounted for with
the underlying melodies of (112). As indicated above, for the first tone of
these melodies there is a three-way contrast—toneless (Ø), Mid (M), or Hi
(H). For the second tone, following any given first tone there are only two
options—Hi and toneless.

(112)   /ØØ/   →   [kùʔì]   'woman's sister'

         /ØH/   →   [vàʔná]   'sleepiness'

         /MØ/   →   [ɲūʔū]   'fire'

         /MH/   →   [bēlú]   'hat'

         /HØ/   →   [tóʔò]   'stranger'

         /HH/   →   [dáʼté]   'is being shorn'

With the exception of *ɲũʔũ* 'fire' and *dáʼté* 'is being shorn', the surface melody of each example in (112) is accounted for in a straightforward manner by the default feature assignment rules. The derivations of *ɲũʔũ* and *dáʼté* are less straightforward. One might expect that if the underlying melody for *ɲũʔũ* is /MØ/, the surface melody for it would be Mid-Lo instead of Mid-Mid. This is, in fact, the case when it is followed by Hi or Mid tone. Consider the examples in (113), in which the first word in each example is from Class A. In (113a, b), when the toneless TBU is followed by Hi or Mid tone, it is assigned Lo tone by default.

(113) a. [ɲũ̄ʔũ̄]   [níʔī]   →   [ɲũ̄ʔũ̀ níʔī]   'flaring fire'
           fire (A)   flaring

           [ʔīt̄ū]   [ní]   →   [ʔītù ní]   'your cornfield'
           cornfield (A)   your

       b. [sākū]   [tē]   →   [sākù tē]   'few of them'
           few (A)   them

           [vīū]   [kʷātī]   →   [vīù kʷātī]   'small cornplants'
           cornplant (A)   small

       c. [ɲū̄ʔū̄]   [vàʔā]   →   [ɲū̄ʔū̄ vàʔā]   'good fire'
           fire (A)   good

In order to account for the final Mid tone of words like *ɲũʔũ* 'fire' and *ʔītū* 'cornfield' when they occur in isolation, or before a Lo tone (toneless TRN), as in (113c), I propose a postlexical rule of Mid Tone Spread.

(114)   Mid Tone Spread (postlexical)

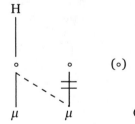

Condition: the optional TRN must be toneless.

In (114), a TRN that dominates a tonal feature *H* spreads rightwards onto a toneless TBU. If the TBU is not utterance-final, a following TRN must also be toneless. The rule must be postlexical because whether it applies or not depends upon what (if anything) follows the target TBU, even if there is an intervening word boundary. Why Mid Tone Spread involves spreading the TRN to the adjacent TBU, as opposed to spreading the feature *H* to the adjacent TRN, is discussed later. The derivation of (113c) appears in (115).

(115)   Underlying form   Mid Tone Spread

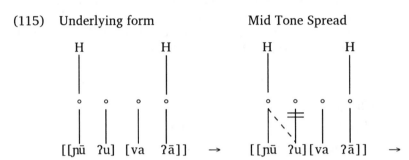

Def. feat. ass., Stray Erasure

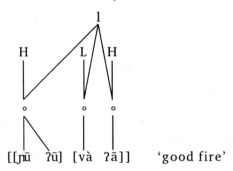

[[ɲū̀ ʔū] [và ʔā]]   'good fire'

In (115), the target of Mid Tone Spread (i.e., *ʔu*) is not utterance final. The TRN that follows it, however (i.e., *va*), is toneless, and so Mid Spread applies. We now return to the assumption made in chapter 2 that adjacent TRNs that meet the structural description of the same default feature assignment rule are assigned the same default feature. In (115), if each toneless TRN were assigned a unique *l*, downstep would occur at the juncture of each toneless TRN, according to the present model. Since this does not happen, I assume that adjacent TRNs like this are assigned the same default feature.

The remaining example in (112) that is not accounted for by the default assignment of features is *dá'té* 'is being shorn'. I analyze the "U" tone in Acatlán Mixtec as a Hi tone that has been "automatically" upstepped following another Hi tone. The derivation of *dá'té* appears in (116). In order to facilitate comparing my representations with those of Pike and Wistrand, I provide their tones immediately below the segmental information in the examples that follow.

(116)   Underlying form   Def. *H* assignment

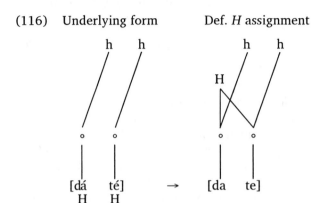

Phonetic representation

'is being shorn'

In Section 6.3 I demonstrated that the OCP is not invoked for tone in Acatlán Mixtec. If the OCP is not a factor, then the occurrence of upstep in (116) can be explained simply by positing adjacent Hi tones underlyingly, with upstep occurring automatically as a result of the register *h*'s being adjacent.

6.3 Upstep

Support for the analysis of the preceding section and the assertion that the OCP is not invoked in Acatlán Mixtec, comes from environments in which upstep occurs when Hi tones are adjacent across word boundaries.

(117) [kó]   [kǎʔǎ]   [nè] → [kó ꜛkǎʔǎ nè] 'he does not speak'

       NEG   speaks   3S

       [kó]   [yúꜛʔí]   [ní] → [kó ꜛyúꜛʔíꜛní] 'you do not fear'

       NEG   fears   2S

       [kʷítá]   [ní] → [kʷìtáꜛní]   'you will be weak'

       will^be^weak   2S

Commenting on the forms in (117), Pike and Wistrand conclude
(1974:96), "The initial tone H of a basic allomorph (of any morpheme
class) becomes U when it contiguously follows H or U (of any morpheme
class)." The fact that upstep always occurs at the juncture of two Hi tones
whenever they are brought into adjacency across word boundaries would
seem to indicate that the OCP does *not* apply across word boundaries in
Acatlán Mixtec. These examples strengthen the claim (made above) that
the occurrence of upstep within words is also due to the presence of adjacent Hi tones that are not subject to OCP constraints. This next example
demonstrates the (theoretically) unlimited terracing that is possible when
Hi tones are juxtaposed.[35]

(118) [kó]   [číꜛtú] [wá] [ní]   [méè] →
       NEG   kisses   so   2S   baby

       [kó   ꜛčíꜛtú   ꜛwá   ꜛní   ꜛméè]
        3   4 5   6   7   8 1
       'you don't kiss the baby so much'

The Hi tone that is upstepped when it follows another Hi across a word
boundary need not necessarily be associated to the first TBU of the second
word. A rule of Hi-Spread, formalized in (119), can also bring two Hi tones
into adjacency on the TBU tier.

---

[35]In this example, Pike and Wistrand assign a phonetic pitch-level of 1 to the final TBU
of the utterance, as opposed to a (perhaps) expected 6. One possible explanation for this,
suggested to me by David Odden (personal communication), is that in Acatlán Mixtec the
tonal register is reset to its default setting at each occurrence of a surface Lo tone. In this
respect it is different from most other languages, which reset the tonal register at the beginning of each new phonological phrase.

(119)   Hi-Spread (postlexical)

Hi-Spread spreads a *h* register feature rightwards across a word boundary onto the first TRN of a following word provided that the target TRN is
not already specified for *h* register (i.e., the target TBU is associated to a
Mid or Lo tone). The examples in (120) demonstrate Hi-Spread in non-
upstepping environments.

(120)   a.   [sà]   [sàʔnú]   [nè]   → [sà sàʔnú né] 'they are old now'
             CONT   old   3P

        b.   [ʔĩ́í]   [dàà]   → [ʔĩ́í dââ]   'stands straight'
             stands   straight

(120a) shows that Hi-Spread can apply when the target TRN is in utterance
final position, and (120b) shows that Hi-Spread affects only the first TRN
of the second word, the final Lo tone being supplied by default. In this next
example, Hi-Spread creates the upstep environment.

(121)   Underlying form   Hi-Spread

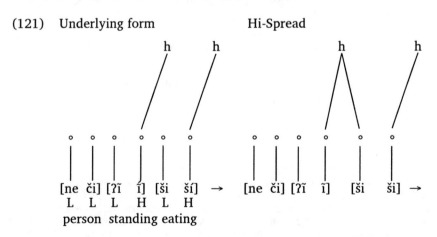

Default feature assignment   Phonetic representation

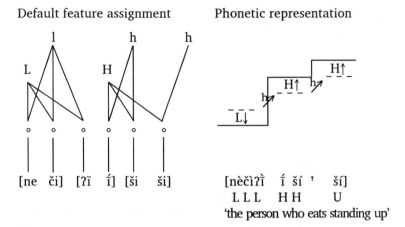

[ne či] [ʔĩ í] [ši   ši]   [nèčìʔĩ̀ í̋ ší ꜛ ší]
                                        L L L   H H   U
                                      'the person who eats standing up'

Hi-Spread brings the two Hi tones into adjacency with respect to the TBU tier. Because the final two TBUs are associated to distinct *h*s, the final TBU is upstepped relative to the TBU that precedes it.

We return to why *l*, rather than *h*, is unspecified in underlying representations, and why the default assignment of *l* is postlexical, rather than lexical. I argue that the OCP is not invoked in Acatlán Mixtec because upstep occurs at each juncture of juxtaposed Hi tones. By the same token, if *l*s were present at any point in a derivation prior to the postlexical component, one would expect downstep to occur (at least across word boundaries) at each juncture of juxtaposed underlying Lo tones. But since this does not happen, cf. (122), I conclude that Lo tones are not present in underlying structures.[36]

(122) a. [tè]   [sà̰ʔnú]   →   [tè sà̰ʔnú] 'the old man'
            3S   old

       b. [ʔùì] [ñà]   →   [ʔùì ñà]   'two of them'
            two   thing (pron)

---

[36]Pike and Wistrand do describe "a general drift downward whereby in relaxed speech, each low tone is usually lower than a preceding low" (1974:84), but the fact that they do not indicate this in any way in their representations suggests that it is not as significant as upstep, which is represented. I attribute this drift downward to phonetic declination, the general tendency for pitch to decline gradually over the course of an utterance (cf. Ladd 1984). It is precisely phenomena like this that are a legitimate domain for the phonetics component to handle (cf. the discussion in §8.2).

So far, we have looked only at examples of Hi-Spread in which the *h* that undergoes the spreading is associated. Hi-Spread also occurs when the TRN that dominates an *h* is floating. This leads us to consider the behavior of Class C words.

Class C words, in contradistinction to Class A words, cause following Lo and Mid-toned TBUs to be realized with surface Hi tones. Consider the examples in (123).

(123)   a. [kwà?à]   [kù?ì]   → [kwà?à kú?ì] 'many sisters'
            many (C)   sister

        b. [kwà?à]   [dè?ē]   → [kwà?à dé?ē] 'many children'
            many (C)   child

        c. [dī?ī]   [zìkū]   → [dī?ī zíkū]   'mother who will sew'
            mother (C) will^sew

In each of these examples, the first word is from Class C, and the second word begins with a Lo tone when it is pronounced in isolation. Following Class C words, however, the second word begins with Hi tone. I analyze all Class C words as ending in a floating Hi tone. Here is the derivation for (123c).

(124)   Underlying form[37]   Hi-Spread

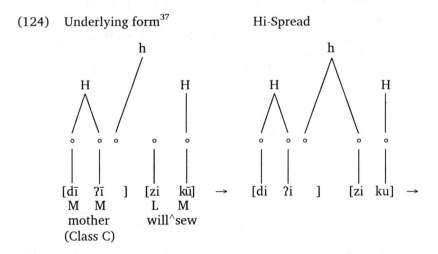

---

[37]Given the assumption that Lo tones in Acatlán Mixtec are underlying unspecified, and given the Mid-Spread rule in (114), which spreads a Mid tone onto a following toneless TBU, the underlying representation of *dī?ī* in (124) as Mid associated to two TBUs is suspect. How do we know that the underlying *dī?ī* is not Mid-toneless, as it is for Class A words that have the melody Mid-Mid when spoken in isolation? The situation in Class C does not completely parallel that of

Default feature assignment, Stray Erasure

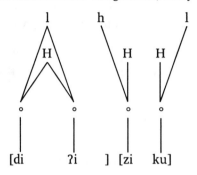

Phonetic representation

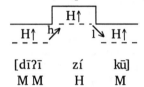

[dī?ī   zí   kū]
 M M   H   M   'mother who will sew'

In the underlying form in (124), there is a floating *h* at the right edge of the first word, and the TRN at the left edge of the second word is unspecified for tonal register. This environment meets the structural description of Hi-Spread, which spreads the *h* onto the toneless TRN. The default rules then assign *l* register features to the remaining TRNs that are unspecified for register. The default rules also assign the tonal feature *H* to the TRN of *zi* as an enhancement to that TRN's *h* register.

When the spreading of a floating Class C *h* brings two *hs* into adjacency with respect to the TBU tier, upstep occurs. Consider (125).

Class A. First, the melody Mid-Mid in Class C words never alternates with Mid-Lo in any environment, as it does in Class A. This argues against assigning the underlying melody Mid-toneless to these words. Secondly, the surface melody Mid-Mid contrasts with the surface melody Mid-Lo in Class C words (cf. *?ī̃* 'hail' and *?ĩ̀* 'skin'). It is, in fact, words like *?ĩ̃* that have the underlying melody Mid-toneless in Class C. Why do words like *?ĩ̃* not undergo Mid-Spread? The reason is that they end in a floating Hi tone and, therefore, do not meet the structural description of the rule. Recall that for Mid-Spread to apply, if the target TBU is not utterance-final, a following TRN must also be toneless. I, therefore, conclude that Class C words with the isolation melody Mid-Mid are best analyzed as having an underlying melody of Mid tone associated to two TBUs.

(125)   Underlying form   Hi-Spread

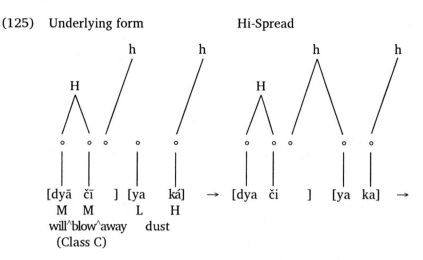

[dyā čī] [ya ká] → [dya či] [ya ka] →
 M M   L   H
will^blow^away   dust
(Class C)

Default feature assignment, Stray Erasure

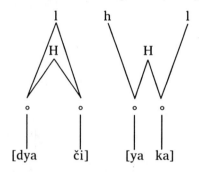

[dya   či]   [ya ka]

Phonetic representation

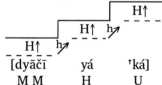

[dyāčī   yá   ⁱká]   'the dust will blow away'
 M M   H   U

The derivation for this example parallels that of the preceding example except that in this case, the application of Hi-Spread brings two *hs* into adjacency on the TBU tier, and upstep occurs.

One possible alternative to this analysis is that the floating Hi tone simply upsteps everything to its right, i.e., the surface tone of *yáⁱká* in (125) is simply the sequence Lo-Hi upstepped. However, if what Pike and Wistrand transcribe as "H U" in this environment were indeed an upstepped Lo-Hi sequence, one would expect the corresponding Lo-Mid sequence in (124) to also be upstepped, and to be transcribed perhaps as "H Half-U." Since Pike and Wistrand transcribe the sequence in (124) as "H M," an analysis that simply upsteps the tonal register at the point of a floating Hi does not work.

When Hi-Spread applies, it is not imperative that the target of Hi-Spread, i.e., the first TRN of the second word, be toneless. It is only necessary that the target be unspecified for h register. As this next example shows, the first tone of the second word can also be Mid.

(126)   [kùmì]   [yāvī]   →   [kùmì yáví]   'four graveholes'
        four (C)   gravehole (A)

The derivation of (126) appears in (127).

(127)   Underlying form   Hi-Spread, Mid Tone Spread

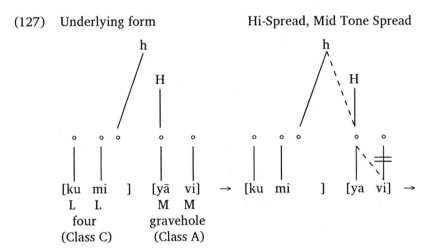

Default feature assignment, Stray Erasure

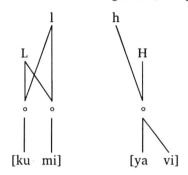

[ku mi]   [ya   vi]

Phonetic representation

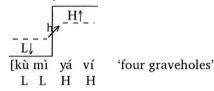

[kù mì yá ví   'four graveholes'
   L   L   H   H

In (127), the underlying melody for *yāvī* is Mid-toneless. The underlying floating *h* at the right edge of the first word spreads rightwards across the word boundary onto the first TRN of *yavi*, and the first TRN of *yavi*, in turn, spreads rightwards onto the adjacent toneless TBU (as a result of Mid Tone Spread). As a result, both TBUs of *yavi* are realized with surface Hi tone.

The derivation in (127) also shows why I claim that the rule of Mid Tone Spread spreads the TRN to the following TBU, as opposed to spreading the feature *H* to the following TRN. If the target of Mid Tone Spread were the TRN, the application of Hi-Spread would affect only the first TBU of *yavi*. This is because Hi-Spread spreads the *h* to only the first TRN, and this TRN would now be dominated only by the first TBU. This may be seen in (128).

(128)   Hi-Spread, Mid Tone Spread (hypothetical)

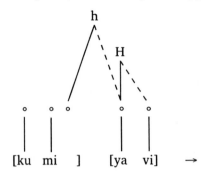

Default feature assignment, Stray Erasure

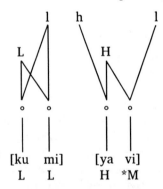

Spreading of the feature *H* to the following TRN would result in the sur-face melody of the final word being Hi-Mid, instead of Hi-Hi.

When Class C words with Mid tone are juxtaposed, upstep occurs (as ex-pected) at each word juncture due to spreading of the floating Hi tones. The example in (129) demonstrates the unlimited nature of the terracing that is possible when this happens. The ascending integers that appear be-low the surface representation indicate ascending levels of pitch.

(129)   [mà]   [kōkō]   [yū̄a]   [dī?ī]   [mī̄ī]   [tē]   [?ī̄ī]
        NEG   will^swallow   father mother   spec.   3S   hail   →

        (C)   (C)   (C)   (C)   (C)   (C)   (C)

        [mà   kókó   ⁺yúá   ⁺dí?í   ⁺míí   ⁺té   ⁺?íí]
         1   3 3   44   5 5   6 6   7   8 8
        'His parents will not swallow the hail.'

This concludes the study of upstep in Acatlán Mixtec. Perhaps the greatest contribution this study makes to phonological theory is the documentation of an upstep system that mirrors so closely the typical downstep systems. Some treatments of register phenomena make no provision for upstep systems (e.g., Clark 1993, Pierrehumbert 1980), due either to limitations inherent in the models assumed or simply to a lack of belief in their existence. The following quotation from Clements' review of Van der Hulst and Snider (1993) is illustrative. I have italicized the relevant parts of the quotation.

> The treatment of upstep, which receives much attention in this volume, remains a particularly difficult problem. A fair amount of evidence suggests that something like upstep, viewed as the contrary of downstep and distinct from mere "resetting" at the end of downstep domains, does exist; yet upstep is not symmetrical to downstep. For example, as just mentioned it is apparently restricted to H tones, and it is *not so far known to be lexically distinctive*. Furthermore, *upstep is not known to apply recursively to create rising intonational staircases*, at least in African languages; this means that any model allowing unbounded upstep must arbitrarily stipulate constraints that conspire to exclude two successive upsteps not separated by downstep. (Clements 1996:851–52)

Acatlán Mixtec provides counter-evidence to two of Clements' claims. First, upstep *is* lexically distinctive. Secondly, upstep *does* apply recursively to create rising intonational staircases. The proviso pertaining to African languages notwithstanding, this calls for a theoretical framework that treats upstep in a manner similar to downstep, with binary features and phonological rules.

7

Downstepped Lo in
Bamileke-Dschang

The studies in earlier chapters have shown that downstep of Hi tones often occurs in the environment of floating Lo tones. This study of Bamileke-Dschang (BD) also demonstrates that downstep of Hi tones occurs in the environment of floating Lo's. In addition, it demonstrates that downstep of Lo tones occurs in the environment of floating Hi's. Bamileke-Dschang, a Grassfields Bantu language spoken in Cameroon, has a very rich variety of surface tonal contrasts, due in part to the fact that there is a relatively large number of floating tones, including Hi, in underlying forms as well as in derived forms. We focus on the associative construction.

The associative construction, which translates 'N$_1$ of N$_2$', consists of a head noun followed by a genitive complement. The genitive complement, in turn, consists of a vocalic associative marker (AM) followed by a second noun. The associative marker is concordant with the head noun, and is underlyingly è when the head noun is from class 1 or 9, á when from class 7, and é when from all other classes. It frequently assimilates to the vowel quality of the preceding vowel and is often deleted in normal conversation. The noun in BD usually consists of a stem and a Lo-toned monosyllabic noun class prefix (NC), although there are a few nouns in classes 1 and 9 which do not take a prefix. At the lexical level then, the grammatical word can be represented as [(prefix) [stem]].

Postlexically, things are slightly different. Hyman (1985) argues convincingly that there is a mismatch between lexical grammatical words and postlexical phonological words in BD. He claims that whereas the nominal grammatical word is stem-final (i.e., head-final), the phonological word is stem-initial (i.e., head-initial) and that it consists of a stem and everything to its right up until the next stem. The observance of such a mismatch is not without precedent in African languages. Hyman draws support from Paulian's (1974) observation of a similar phenomenon in Kukuya. More recently, mismatches between morphological and prosodic domains have been documented for Igbo (Zsiga 1992), Shona (Myers 1995), and Ejagham (Watters 1997). Following Hyman then, the phonological nominal word in BD is best represented postlexically as [[stem] AM (prefix)]. Prefixes of the first word in an utterance are considered extraprosodic.

7.1 Noun tone classes

The BD noun root is usually monosyllabic, although disyllabic roots do exist. For monosyllabic roots, Hyman and Tadadjeu (1976) posit the four underlying structures of (130a) and demonstrate that they derive from the respective Proto-Mbam-Nkam structures of (130b).

(130)   Noun root structures

a. Bamileke-Dschang   CÝ   CV̂   CV̀   CV̀́

b. Proto-Mbam-Nkam   *CÝCÝ   *CÝCV̀   *CV̀CV̀   *CV̀CÝ

Most of the data in this chapter come from an instrumental study I have undertaken of the data in Hyman (1985). For the most part, my transcriptions, which are included in the appendix, confirm those of Hyman. The few places where they differ are indicated with an asterisk. Instrumental support for the transcriptions is also provided in the appendix. I assume the correctness of Hyman's underlying representations for the various forms. The noun class a noun belongs to (and hence the associative markers Hyman assumes) are readily determined by the noun's concordant affixes in other (i.e., nonassociative) constructions. Similarly, the tonal class a noun root belongs to can be determined from its isolation form. Examples of the four tonal classes appear in (131) and (132). For (131b, d) and (132b, d), the second tone of the root is floating in underlying forms.

(131)   Noun class prefix + root (isolation form)[38]

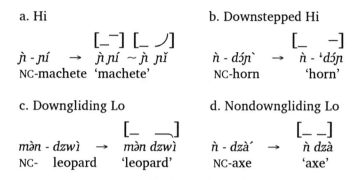

    a. Hi   b. Downstepped Hi

             [‾] [_ ⁄]   [_ ‾]
    ɲ̀ - ɲí   →   *ɲ̀ɲí ~ ɲ̀ ɲǐ*   *ǹ - dɔ́ɲˋ*   →   *ǹ - ꜜdɔ́ɲ*
    NC-machete 'machete'   NC-horn   'horn'

    c. Downgliding Lo   d. Nondowngliding Lo

             [_ ╲]   [_ _]
    màn - dzwì   →   *màn dzwì*   *ǹ - dzàˊ*   →   *ǹ dzà*
    NC- leopard   'leopard'   NC-axe   'axe'

(132)   Root with no noun class prefix (isolation form)

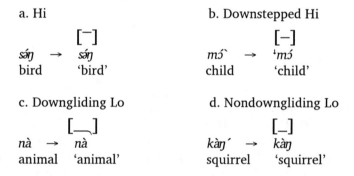

    a. Hi   b. Downstepped Hi

           [‾]   [–]
    sə́ŋ   →   *sə́ŋ*   *mɔ́ˋ*   →   *ꜜmɔ́*
    bird   'bird'   child   'child'

    c. Downgliding Lo   d. Nondowngliding Lo

        [_╲]   [_]
    nà   →   *nà*   *kàŋˊ*   →   *kàŋ*
    animal   'animal'   squirrel   'squirrel'

The Hi and downgliding Lo forms are typical of many African languages: the Hi is pronounced at the highest pitch level, and Lo at the lowest pitch level. Like many African languages, the Lo falls or downglides utterance finally. In this respect, it contrasts with the nondowngliding Lo, which in nonfinal environments is phonetically indistinguishable from the downgliding Lo. As shown below, however, the two Lo's behave quite differently phonologically. Given that the nondowngliding Lo tone derives historically from a disyllabic Lo Hi sequence, I find convincing Hyman and Tadadjeu's analysis of it as a Lo tone followed by a floating Hi. Since utterance-final Lo tones are phonetically realized as falling in many African languages, the fact that the Lo of the nondowngliding Lo is not utterance-final (due to the final floating Hi) provides a reasonable explanation for its failure to downglide.

---

[38]The sequence Lo Hi is optionally realized as Lo Lo-Rising due to a "late L-spreading rule" (Hyman 1985:49).

7.2 Downstepped Hi tones

The downstepped Hi tone in BD is pronounced at a pitch level that is lower than Hi and higher than Lo. Pulleyblank (1986:44, 45) argues that this *is*, in fact, an underlying Hi tone that has subsequently been downstepped, as opposed to being an underlying Mid tone. He shows, for example, that if a downstepped Hi is followed by a normal Hi, the normal Hi is realized at the same pitch as the downstepped Hi.

(133) à-pú`   á   sə̀ŋ   →   [à⁺pú sə́ŋ]   (cf. [à⁺pú] 'arm', [sə̀ŋ] 'bird')
       NC-arm AM bird   'arm of bird'

In (133) the Hi-toned associative marker *á* is deleted in normal speech. Pulleyblank also demonstrates that when a word with downstepped Hi is followed by a second word with downstepped Hi, there is a sequence of downsteps.

(134) à-pú`    á   mɔ̂`   →   [à⁺pú ⁺mɔ́] (cf. [à⁺pú] 'arm', [⁺mɔ́] 'child')
       NC-arm AM child   'arm of child'

Pulleyblank concludes that these facts are unexpected if the lowered tones are phonological Mid tones. A Hi tone after a Mid is normally realized at a pitch level that is higher than the Mid, and a Mid after a Mid is normally realized at the same pitch level as the preceding Mid.

One further argument for analyzing the surface downstepped Hi as an underlying Hi Lo sequence is that in certain environments it behaves like a Hi tone that is followed by a floating Lo, and in certain other environments it behaves like a Lo tone that is preceded by a floating Hi. The first situation is demonstrated in (135) with a verb in its infinitival form. The infinitive in BD is a class 5 (C5) noun and consists of the C5 prefix *lə̀-* and a stem. Tadadjeu (1974:289) demonstrates that the stem, in turn, consists of a verb root and a floating Lo tone infinitive (INF) suffix. Compare the infinitive in (135a) with an ordinary C5 noun in (135b).

(135) a.   lə̀-tɔ́ŋ-`   →   [lə̀⁺tɔ́ŋ] 'to read'
            C5-read-INF
       b.   lə̀-tɔ́ŋ   →   [lə̀tɔ́ŋ] 'feather'
            C5-feather

Tadadjeu also demonstrates that the verb root *tɔ́ŋ* 'read' is underlyingly Hi-toned. In its infinitival form, however, the floating Lo tone of the infinitive suffix causes the Hi tone of the verb root to be downstepped. That the downstep is attributable to the floating Lo suffix and not the Lo-toned prefix may be seen by comparing (135a) with (135b). In (135b), there is no floating Lo tone and hence no downstep. The fact that nouns like à'pú 'arm' behave similarly to infinitives like là'tɔ́ŋ 'to read', with its Hi-toned root and floating Lo suffix, supports the notion that lexically downstepped nouns also have a Hi tone that is followed by a floating Lo.

The second situation in which the tone of lexically downstepped Hi-toned nouns behaves like a Hi Lo sequence is seen in environments where the floating Lo at the right edge of the noun spreads leftwards onto the final TBU of the noun, displacing the original Hi tone. This creates a sequence in which a Lo tone is preceded by a floating Hi. As will be demonstrated, when two Lo tones in BD are separated by a floating Hi, the second Lo is downstepped relative to the first Lo. This is most easily demonstrated with examples like (136), in which all tones are Lo except for a floating Hi at the right edge of the first word. Recall that Lo-toned words like ǹ-dzà´ 'axe' that end in a floating Hi tone are easily distinguished in isolation from their Lo-toned counterparts that do not end in a floating Hi tone by their failure to end in a falling tone.

(136) ǹ-dzà´ è   màn-dzwì   →   [ǹdzà 'màndzwì] 'axe of leopards'
       NC-axe AM NC-leopard

In (136) the Lo tones to the right of the floating Hi are downstepped relative to the Lo tones to the left of the floating Hi. There is also a vowel deletion rule that deletes the associative marker in normal speech. This rule is not formalized in the present work, but it does play a role in the derivations that follow. Now consider an example like (137) in which the only Hi tone in the utterance is that of the first word.

(137) ǹ-dɔ́ŋ`   è   màn-dzwì   →   [ǹ'dɔ̀ŋ màndzwì] 'horn of leopards'
       NC-horn AM NC-leopard

I will argue below that within phonological words, when an associated Lo tone follows a Hi floating Lo sequence, as in (137), the floating Lo spreads leftward and delinks the Hi tone from its TBU. This creates the environment in which Lo tones after the floating Hi are downstepped relative to Lo tones before the floating Hi. If words like ǹ'dɔ́ŋ 'horn' and à'pú 'arm' are underlyingly Mid-toned, there is no reason, a priori, for them to behave phonologically in the same manner as constructions whose tones are obviously sequences of Hi Lo.

I account for the downstepping of Hi in words like ǹ'dɔ́ŋ 'horn' and à'pú 'arm' with a rule of Lexical Leftwards l-Spread, formalized in (138). This

rule includes "lexical" in its name in order to distinguish it from another
similar postlexical rule (discussed later).

(138)   Lexical Leftwards *l*-Spread

In (138), when a Hi tone is followed by a floating *l*, the floating *l* spreads
leftwards and delinks the *h* from its TRN. Lexical Leftwards *l*-Spread is demonstrated in (139). The present work assumes that only two underlying tone
features are necessary in BD, *h* and *l*, and that lexical default rules fill in all unspecified tonal values prior to the application of Lexical Leftwards *l*-Spread.

(139)   Underlying form   Default Feature Assignment (lexical)

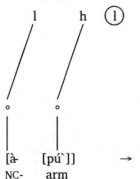   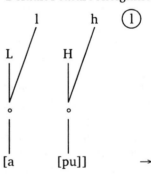

Lexical Leftwards *l*-Spread   Stray Erasure (postlexical)

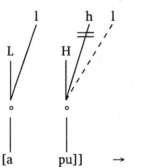   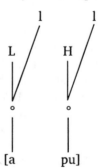

Phonetic representation

$$\overline{\text{L}\downarrow\;\text{l}\!\!\backslash\;\text{H}\uparrow}$$

[à   ꜜpú]   'arm'

In this example the floating *l* has spread leftwards to the TRN of the preceding Hi tone and delinked the *h* from that TRN. The second (Hi-toned) TBU is now realized on a lower register, i.e., it is downstepped.

Pulleyblank's first reason for assuming that the final tone of à꜐pú is a downstepped Hi as opposed to a Mid tone is that when there is a Hi tone following, the second Hi is also downstepped to the level of the preceding tone. I account for this with a postlexical rule of Rightwards *l*-Spread, formalized in (140).

(140)   Rightwards *l*-Spread (postlexical, iterative)

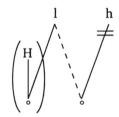

Whenever a floating *l* or a *l* that is coassociated with *H* precedes *h* on the Register tier, the *l* spreads rightwards and delinks the *h* from its TRN. Like the *l*-Spread rule of many African languages, this rule applies iteratively. This ensures that a Hi tone or any sequence of Hi tones that follows a floating Lo or a previously downstepped Hi tone will be downstepped. Motivation for Rightwards *l*-Spread being triggered by a previously downstepped Hi tone comes from examples like (141), in which underlyingly Hi-toned *sə́ŋ* 'bird' is downstepped to the level of the lexically downstepped à꜐pú 'arm' that precedes it. Motivation for Rightwards *l*-Spread being triggered by floating Lo's is provided further below. The reader will note that the derivation in (141) is entirely postlexical.

(141)   Output of lexical phonology   Phon. Word Formation, OCP

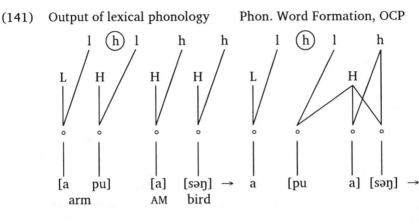

Rightwards *l*-Spread   V-Deletion, Stray Erasure

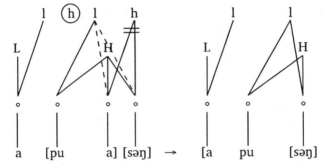

Phonetic representation

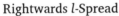

[à   'pú sə́ŋ]   'arm of bird'

In this example the floating *l* at the end of the first word has spread left-wards lexically, previous to this derivation (cf. the derivation in (139)). In the postlexical phonology, phonological words are derived as described above, and this is indicated by the changes in bracketing on the segmental tier. The *l* of the lexically downstepped Hi spreads rightwards to the TRNs of the following Hi tones and delinks the *h*s from those TRNs. Following this, Vowel Deletion and Stray Erasure apply. The final two TBUs of the ut-terance are, therefore, phonetically realized at the same (downstepped) pitch level.

Pulleyblank's second reason for assuming that the final tone of à'pú is a downstepped Hi as opposed to a Mid tone is that when a word with downstepped Hi is followed by a second word with downstepped Hi, there is a sequence of downsteps. The derivation in (142) shows how this is accounted for in Register Tier Theory.

(142)   Output of lexical phonology

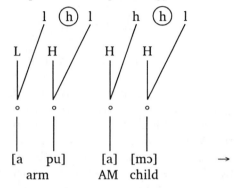

[a   pu]   [a]   [mɔ]   →
      arm   AM   child

Phonological Word Formation, OCP

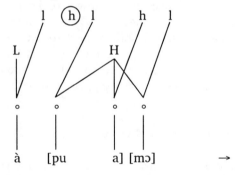

à   [pu   a]   [mɔ]   →

V-Deletion, Stray Erasure   Phonetic representation

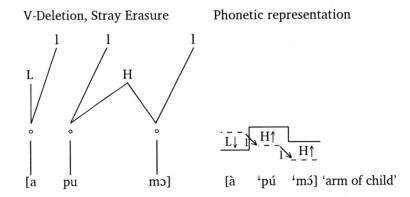

[a   pu   mɔ]   [à   ꜛpú   ꜛmɔ́] 'arm of child'

In this example the underlying floating *l*s at the end of each word have spread leftwards lexically (previous to this derivation) and created the floating *h*s that appear in the input to this derivation. Postlexically, following application of Phonological Word Formation and the OCP, Vowel Deletion deletes the vowel of the associative marker causing the *h* that was associated to it to float. Stray Erasure then deletes all unassociated elements. Interpreting the resulting structural representation, we note that each TBU is associated to a unique register feature *l*. This means that each TBU is phonetically realized on a succeedingly lower register. The first TBU of the utterance is Lo-toned with respect to its register, and the final two TBUs of the utterance are Hi-toned with respect to their registers. Since the second Hi tone is realized on a lower register than the first Hi tone, it is, therefore, downstepped relative to the first. We turn our attention now from downstepped Hi tones to downstepped Lo tones.

7.3 Downstepped Lo tones

All instances of downstepped Lo tones in the BD associative construction involve one or other of the three environments in (143), and for each environment I show that the downstep is attributable to a floating Hi.

(143)   Underlying environments that result in downstepped Lo's in BD

        a. Lo-toned stems that end with a floating Hi (e.g., ǹdzà ´ 'axe')
        b. Hi-toned stems that end with a floating Lo (e.g., ǹdɔ́ŋ` 'horn')
        c. Lo-toned stems followed by a Hi-toned associative marker (e.g., àzɔ́b á 'song of')

In the case of (143a), the Hi is already floating and does not need to be derived. In (143b), the floating Hi is derived by the independent leftwards spreading of the register and tone features of the floating Lo tone and consequent delinking of the respective features of the Hi tone. And in (143c), the floating Hi is derived by the rightwards spreading of the Lo tone from the preceding noun. We now examine examples from each of these environments in which all underlying tones are Lo except for the Hi in question.

The first environment that results in downstepped Lo's in BD (143a) is relatively straightforward. In (144) all underlying tones are Lo except for the *h* at the right edge of the first noun root. This *h* is a nonderived floating tone, i.e., it is not floating as a result of any spread/delink process.

(144)   Underlying form   OCP (lexical), Output of lexical level

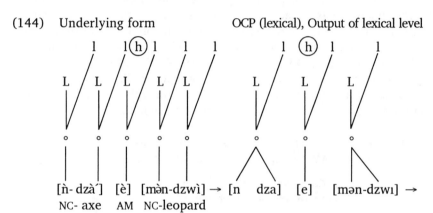

[ǹ- dzà́] [è] [mə̀n-dzwì] → [n   dza]   [e]   [mən-dzwɪ] →
NC- axe   AM   NC-leopard

Phon. Wd. Form., OCP, V-Assim.   Stray Erasure

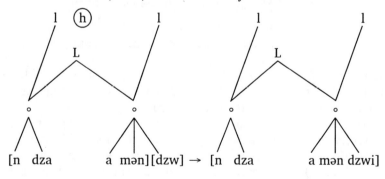

[n   dza   a   mən] [dzw] → [n   dza   a   mən dzwi]

Phonetic representation

[ǹdzà ꜛà mə̀n dzwì]   'axe of leopards'

Apart from the OCP and Phonological Word Formation, the only rule that applies in (144) is Vowel Assimilation (not formalized). The OCP cannot merge the two register *l*s because there is an intervening *h* on the Register tier; consequently, the second Lo is downstepped relative to the first Lo.

The downstepping of Lo tones in BD is cumulative, i.e., a sequence of downstepped Lo's is terraced, much the same as it is for downstepped Hi tones. This is demonstrated in (145) with repetitions of words from the environment discussed immediately above (viz., Lo-toned roots that end with a floating Hi). (145a) involves the sequencing of *ǹ-dzà'* from (144), and (145b) involves the sequencing of *kàŋ'* 'squirrel'. Like *ǹ-dzà'*, *kàŋ'* is pronounced with a nondowngliding Lo tone in isolation and belongs to Class 9, which means it also takes the associative marker *è-*.[39]

(145)   a. *ǹ-dzà'   è   ǹ-dzà'   è   ǹ-dzà'   è   ǹ-dzà'*   →
        NC-axe AM NC-axe AM NC-axe AM NC-axe

        [ǹdzà ꜛǹdzà ꜛǹdzà ꜛǹdzà]
        'axe of axe of axe of axe'

        b. *kàŋ'   è   kàŋ'   è   kàŋ'   è   kàŋ'*   →
        squirrel AM squirrel AM squirrel AM squirrel

        [kàŋ ꜛkàŋ ꜛkàŋ ꜛkàŋ]
        'squirrel of squirrel of squirrel of squirrel'

From these examples it is clear that the downstepping of Lo tones in BD can involve more than one TBU, and can involve terracing (i.e., the phenomenon in question is truly downstep).

The second environment that results in downstepped Lo's in BD, (143b), involves the leftwards spreading of the floating Lo tone and consequent delinking of the Hi. Two rules, Lexical Leftwards *l*-Spread, formalized in (138), and Feature *L*-Spread, formalized in (146), conspire to accomplish this.

---

[39]I elicited these data (with gratitude) from Professor Maurice Tadadjeu, the original source of the data in Hyman and Tadadjeu (1976).

(146)   Feature *L*-Spread

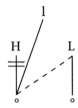

Condition: The first TRN must be singly-linked.

In (146), a feature *L* spreads leftwards and delinks a preceding tonal feature *H* when the TBU bearing that *H* is associated to a register *l*. The constraint against the first TRN being multiply-linked is necessary in order to rule out applications of the rule to forms like (147).

(147)   à-láʔ`   á màn-dzwì → [àˈláʔ á mə́ndzwì] 'country of leopards'
         NC-country AM NC-leopard

If there were no constraint against the first TRN in (146) being multiply-linked, Rightwards *l*-Spread would create the environment in (147) for Feature *L*-Spread to apply, with the result that the *L* of the final Lo tone of the utterance would spread leftwards.

Example (148) meets the structural descriptions of both (138) and (146). All underlying tones are Lo except for the Hi on the second TBU. In the underlying form there is a floating *l* to the right of this Hi. In the lexical component, the floating *l* spreads leftwards onto the TRN of *dɔŋ* and delinks the *h* of that node. The output of the lexical component forms the input to (148).

(148)   Output of lexical component   Phon. Wd. Formation, OCP

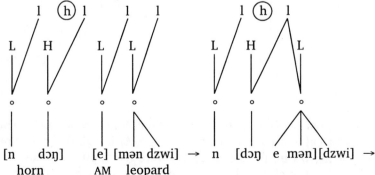

Feature *L*-Spread, V-Del.   Stray Erasure

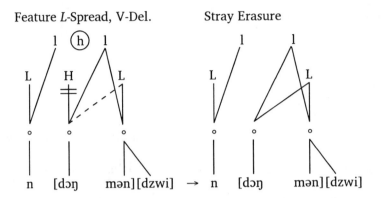

n   [dɔŋ   mən][dzwi]   →   n   [dɔŋ   mən][dzwi]

Phonetic representation

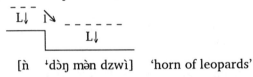

[ǹ   ⁱdɔŋ mə̀n dzwì]   'horn of leopards'

In (148), the postlexical rule of Feature *L*-Spread spreads the *L* of the second word leftwards also onto the TRN of *dɔŋ* and dissociates the *H* of that node. The floating *h* blocks application of the OCP to the two *l*s, and this results in the second Lo being downstepped relative to the first Lo.

The third environment that results in downstepped Lo's in BD, (143c), invokes three rules: a postlexical rule of Hi Tone Spread (HTS), and two postlexical rules of Lo Tone Spread. The rule of HTS is formalized in (149).

(149)   Hi Tone Spread (HTS) (postlexical)

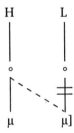

HTS spreads a Hi tone from its TRN onto the final Lo-toned TBU of the phonological word, delinking the Lo tone. Although the rule is restricted to applying within the phonological word (stem plus all material up to a following stem; cf. the discussion in the introductory paragraphs of this

chapter), it applies nevertheless postlexically (following postlexical Phonological Word Formation). Compare the examples in (150), which justify
the rule of HTS independently of the downstepping environment.

(150) a. à-*sáŋ*   á *mə̀n-dzwì*   → [àsáŋ á mə́ndzwì] 'tail of leopards'
          NC-tail AM NC-leopard

      b. ɲ̀-*ɲí*   è *mèn-dzwì* → [ɲ̀ɲǐ mə̀ndzwì] 'machete of leopards'
          NC-machete AM NC-leopard

      c. à-*sáŋ*   á *nà*   → [àsáŋ á nà] 'tail of animal'
          NC-tail AM animal

In (150a) the Hi of the associative marker spreads onto the noun class prefix of the second noun. This may be contrasted with (150b) in which the Hi
does not spread onto the associative marker because the associative
marker is not the final TBU of the phonological word. It may also be
contrasted with (150c). In (150c), the Hi of the associative marker does
not spread across a word boundary onto the stem of the following word.

    It was stated above that there were three rules invoked in the third envi-
ronment that results in downstepped Lo's. The second, Postlexical Lo Tone
Spread 1, is formalized in (151).

(151)   Lo Tone Spread 1 (LTS1) (postlexical)

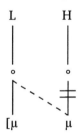

In (151) the first Lo tone of a phonological word spreads rightwards from
its TRN and delinks a following Hi tone from its TBU. This is demonstrated
in (152) in an environment that is independent of the downstepping
phenomenon.

(152)   à-z*ɔ̀b*   á *sə́ŋ*   →   [à-zɔ̀b ɔ̀ sə́ŋ]   'song of bird'
          NC-song AM bird

The third rule that plays a role in the third environment that results in downstepped Lo's is Postlexical Lo Tone Spread 2, formalized in (153).

(153)   Lo Tone Spread 2 (LTS2) (postlexical)

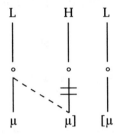

LTS2 spreads a Lo tone rightwards to the final TBU of the phonological word and delinks a Hi tone from that TBU. This only happens if the following word begins with Lo tone.

Now look at (154), which meets the structural descriptions of HTS and both LTS rules.

(154)   Output of lexical component

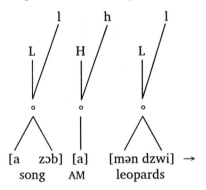

Phon. Wd. Form., HTS, LTS1, V-Ass.

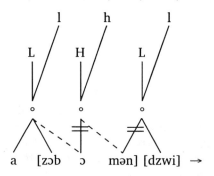

a   [zɔb   ɔ   mən] [dzwi]   →

LTS2   Stray Erasure

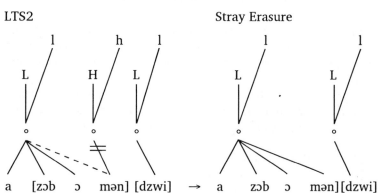

a   [zɔb   ɔ   mən] [dzwi]   →   a   zɔb   ɔ   mən][dzwi]

Phonetic representation

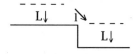

[àzɔ̀b ɔ̀ mə̀n ꜜdzwì]   'song of leopards'

In (154) the output of Phonological Word Formation meets the structural descriptions of both HTS and LTS1. HTS, in turn, feeds LTS2, which causes the only Hi tone in the utterance to float. The floating Hi tone prevents OCP constraints from coalescing the two Lo tones that exist at the end of the derivation with the result that the tone of the TBU associated with the second Lo is downstepped relative to that associated with the first TBU.

This brings us to the conclusion of the study of downstepped Lo tones in BD. All instances of downstepped Lo tones in the BD associative construction involve one or other of three environments, and in each environment, the downstep is attributable to the existence of a floating Hi tone between Lo tones.

7.4 Additional data

Following the presentation of any linguistic analysis, the question arises whether the analysis also holds for data that is not included in the presentation. In principle, the question can always be asked, regardless of how much data is covered. However, since derivations for only a relatively few examples have been provided, the reader will find it helpful to be able to extend the study. Appendix A includes a summary of the rules needed to account for the data. Appendix B includes phonetic transcriptions (with instrumental support) for the complete set of possible tone combinations of disyllabic nouns in the BD associative construction.[40] Then for each of the thirty-two examples, there is a listing of the rules that apply in the order that they apply.

Given the rules already presented above, only one more rule is needed in order to account for the examples of the extended study. That rule is Postlexical Leftwards *l*-Spread, formalized in (155).

(155)   Postlexical Leftwards *l*-Spread

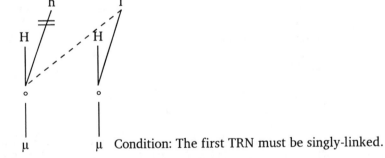

Condition: The first TRN must be singly-linked.

Whenever a lexically downstepped Hi tone is preceded by a singly-linked Hi tone, the register feature *l* of the downstepped Hi spreads leftwards onto the TRN of the preceding Hi tone and delinks the register

---

[40]Hyman's (1985) study also accounts for the different possible tone combinations of monosyllabic nouns. However, the additional discussion that would be required in order to account for monosyllabic nouns in this presentation would not significantly further the contribution the BD study makes to the greater work.

feature *h* of that Hi tone. Justification for the singly-linked Hi tone constraint is provided in (157). (155) is demonstrated in this next derivation.

(156)   Output of lexical component   Phon. Wd. Form., HTS, LTS1

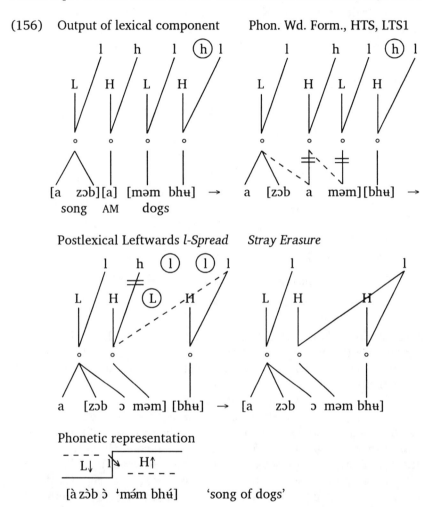

Phonetic representation

[à zɔ̀b ɔ̀ ˈmə́m bhʉ́]   'song of dogs'

Similar to (154), the output of the lexical component in (156) meets the structural description of both HTS and LTS1. Following the application of these rules, the Hi tone is singly-linked to a TBU immediately to the left of a lexically downstepped Hi tone. This, in turn, meets the structural description of Postlexical Leftwards *l*-Spread, which spreads the register feature *l* of the lexically downstepped Hi leftwards onto the TRN of the preceding TBU. In the output of the postlexical component, the first three

TBUs of the utterance are associated to a Lo tone. This, in turn, is followed
by the final two TBUs associated to a downstepped Hi tone.

The constraint against the Hi tone that undergoes Postlexical Leftwards
l-Spread being multiply-linked finds its source in examples like those in
(157). These examples are taken directly from appendix B.

(157)   a. Singly-linked Hi tones

    19. àzɔ̀b á màmbhʉ̌` → àzɔ̀b ɔ̀ ꜜmámbhʉ́ 'song of dogs'

    20. àzɔ̀b á màtsɔ́ŋ → àzɔ̀b ɔ̀ ꜜmátsɔ́ŋ 'song of thieves'

    23. àlàŋ´ á màmbhʉ̌` → àlàŋ à̀ ꜜmámbhʉ́ 'stool of dogs'

    24. àlàŋ´ á màtsɔ́ŋ → àlàŋ à̀ ꜜmátsɔ́ŋ 'stool of thieves'

    b. Multiply-linked Hi tones

    27. àlá?`  á  màmbhʉ̌` → à꜀lá? á mám꜀bhʉ́ 'country of dogs'

    28. àlá?` á màtsɔ́ŋ → à꜀lá? á mə̀꜀tsɔ́ŋ 'country of thieves'

    31. àsáŋ á màmbhʉ̌` → àsáŋ á mám꜀bhʉ́ 'tail of dogs'

    32. àsáŋ á màtsɔ́ŋ → àsáŋ á mə̀꜀tsɔ́ŋ 'tail of thieves'

A comparison of the surface forms of these examples shows that singly-
linked Hi tones that precede downstepped Hi tones are always downstepped
to the level of the following downstepped Hi tones, and that multiply-linked
Hi tones that precede downstepped Hi tones are never downstepped to the
level of the following downstepped Hi tones.

In the typologies presented in chapter 3, a sequence of two Hi tones separated by a floating Lo results in downstep of the second Hi if the register *l*
spreads rightwards, but results in upstep of the second Hi if the *l* remains
floating. Similarly, a sequence of two Lo tones separated by a floating Hi
results in upstep of the second Lo if the register *h* spreads rightwards, but
results in downstep of the second Lo if the *h* remains floating. Whether the
presence of the intervening tone results in downstep or upstep depends
only upon a parameter setting for its register feature—Spread: Yes/No. In
the case of Bamileke-Dschang, the register feature *h* remains floating and
this results in a downstepped Lo tone.

Appendix A: Rules

(138)   Lexical Leftwards *l*-Spread

(140)   Rightwards *l*-Spread (postlexical, iterative)

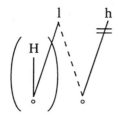

(146)   Feature *l*-Spread

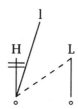

Condition: The first TRN must be singly-linked.

(149)   Hi Tone Spread (HTS) (postlexical)

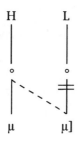

(151)   Lo Tone Spread 1 (LTS1) (postlexical)

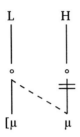

(153)   Lo Tone Spread 2 (LTS2) (postlexical)

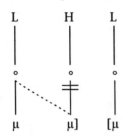

(155)   Postlexical Leftwards *l*-Spread

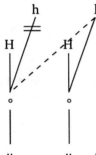

Condition: The first TRN must be singly-linked.

Appendix B: Disyllabic N₁ + disyllabic N₂ in associative construction

The following chart, adapted from Hyman (1985:50), displays my transcriptions for the complete set of possible tone combinations of disyllabic nouns in the BD associative construction. In the four places where my transcriptions differ from those of Hyman, I have also provided Hyman's transcription (indicated with an asterisk). The ° symbol indicates that the final Lo is not falling. It should be kept in mind that Tadadjeu, the source of my data, was not the source of the data in Hyman (1985). Following the gloss of each example, there is a list of the rules that apply, given in the order that they apply.

1.	èfɔ	è mèndzwì	→ èfɔ màndzwì	'chief of leopards' (-)
2.	èfɔ	è mèŋkὺɔʔˊ	→ èfɔ màŋkὺɔʔ°	'chief of roosters' (-)
3.	èfɔ	è mèmbhɻˋ	→ èfɔ màmˈbhɻ	'chief of dogs' (138)
4.	èfɔ	è mètsɔ́ŋ	→ èfɔ màtsɔ̌ŋ	'chief of thieves' (-)
5.	ǹdzàˊ	è màndzwì	→ ǹdzà ˈmàndzwì	'axe of leopards' (-)
*5.	ǹdzàˊ	è màndzwì	→ ǹdzà ˈà màndzwì	'axe of leopards' (Hyman)
6.	ǹdzàˊ	è màŋkὺɔʔˊ	→ ǹdzà ˈmàŋkὺɔʔ°	'axe of roosters' (-)
*6.	ǹdzàˊ	è màŋkὺɔʔˊ	→ ǹdzà ˈà màŋkὺɔʔ°	'axe of roosters' (Hyman)
7.	ǹdzàˊ	è màmbhɻˋ	→ ǹdzà ˈmàmˈbhɻ	'axe of dogs' (138)
*7.	ǹdzàˊ	è màmbhɻˋ	→ ǹdzà ˈà màmˈbhɻ	'axe of dogs' (Hyman)
8.	ǹdzàˊ	è màtsɔ́ŋ	→ ǹdzà ˈmàtsɔ̌ŋ	'axe of thieves' (-)
*8.	ǹdzàˊ	è màtsɔ́ŋ	→ ǹdzà ˈà màtsɔ̌ŋ	'axe of thieves' (Hyman)
9.	ǹdɔ́ŋˋ	è màndzwì	→ ǹˈdɔ̀ŋ màndzwì	'horn of leopards' (138, 146)
10.	ǹdɔ́ŋˋ	è màŋkὺɔʔˊ	→ ǹˈdɔ̀ŋ màŋkὺɔʔ°	'horn of roosters' (138, 146)
11.	ǹdɔ́ŋˋ	è màmbhɻˋ	→ ǹˈdɔ̀ŋ màmˈbhɻ	'horn of dogs' (138, 146)
12.	ǹdɔ́ŋˋ	è màtsɔ́ŋ	→ ǹˈdɔ̀ŋ màtsɔ̌ŋ	'horn of thieves' (138, 146)
13.	ɲɲí	è màndzwì	→ ɲɲǐ màndzwì	'machete of leopards' (-)
14.	ɲɲí	è màŋkὺɔʔˊ	→ ɲɲǐ màŋkὺɔʔ°	machete of roosters' (-)
15.	ɲɲí	è màmbhɻˋ	→ ɲɲǐ màmˈbhɻ	'machete of dogs' (158)
16.	ɲɲí	è màtsɔ́ŋ	→ ɲɲǐ màtsɔ̌ŋ	'machete of thieves' (-)
17.	àzɔ̀b	á màndzwì	→ àzɔ̀b ɔ̀ màⁿˈdzwì	'song of leopards' (149, 151, 153)

18. àzɔ̀b   á màŋkɨ̀ɔʔˊ   → àzɔ̀b ɔ̀ màŋˈkɨ̀ɔʔ°   'song of roosters' (149, 151, 153)

19. àzɔ̀b   á màmbhɨ́ˋ   → àzɔ̀b ɔ̀ ˈmámbhɨ́   'song of dogs' (138, 149, 151, 155)

20. àzɔ̀b   á màtsɔ́ŋ   → àzɔ̀b ɔ̀ ˈmátsɔ́ŋ   'song of thieves' (149, 151, 140, 155)

21. àlə̀ŋˊ   á màndzwì   → àlə̀ŋ ə̀ mànˈdzwì   'stool of leopards' (149, 151, 153)

22. àlə̀ŋˊ   á màŋkɨ̀ɔʔˊ   → àlə̀ŋ ə̀ màŋˈkɨ̀ɔʔ°   'stool of roosters' (149, 151, 153)

23. àlə̀ŋˊ   á màmbhɨ́ˋ   → àlə̀ŋ ə̀ ˈmámbhɨ́   'stool of dogs' (138, 149, 151, 155)

24. àlə̀ŋˊ   á màtsɔ́ŋ   → àlə̀ŋ ə̀ ˈmátsɔ́ŋ   'stool of thieves' (149, 151, 140, 155)

25. àláʔˋ   á màndzwì   → àˈláʔ á mándzwì   'country of leopards' (138, 149, 140)

26. àláʔˋ   á màŋkɨ̀ɔʔˊ   → àˈláʔ á máŋkɨ̀ɔʔ°   'country of roosters' (138, 149, 140)

27. àláʔˋ   á màmbhɨ́ˋ   → àˈláʔ á mámˈbhɨ́   'country of dogs' (138, 149, 140)

28. àláʔˋ   á màtsɔ́ŋ   → àˈláʔ á mə́ˈtsɔ́ŋ   'country of thieves' (138, 149, 140)

29. àsáŋ   á màndzwì   → àsáŋ á mándzwì   'tail of leopards' (149)

30. àsáŋ   á màŋkɨ̀ɔʔˊ   → àsáŋ á máŋkɨ̀ɔʔ°   'tail of roosters' (149)

31. àsáŋ   á màmbhɨ́ˋ   → àsáŋ á mámˈbhɨ́   'tail of dogs' (138, 149)

32. àsáŋ   á màtsɔ́ŋ   → àsáŋ á mə́ˈtsɔ́ŋ   'tail of thieves' (149, 140)

Appendix C: Pitch traces for associative construction

These pitch traces come from an instrumental study I have undertaken of the examples of the BD associative construction provided in Hyman (1985). The study is based on audio recordings that Steven Bird made of Prof. Maurice Tadadjeu, the original source of the data in Hyman and Tadadjeu (1976). I am grateful to Steven for having made these recordings available to me. Steven's own instrumental work on these recordings is published in Bird and Stegen (1995), and digitized renditions of the recordings themselves are available on the internet at http://www.cogsci.ed.ak.uk/~steven. In the phonetic transcriptions, the characters were placed at the beginning of their respective sounds.

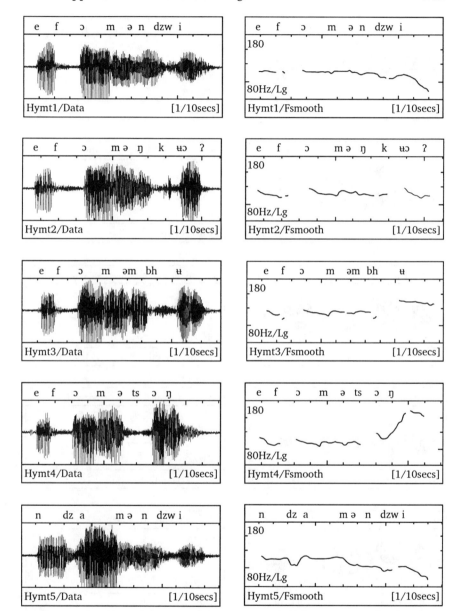

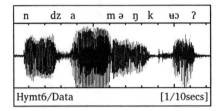

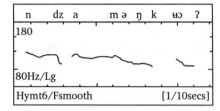

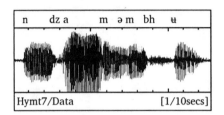

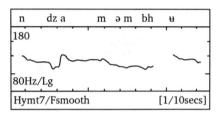

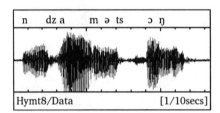

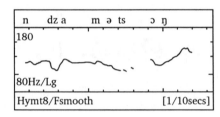

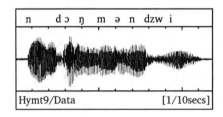

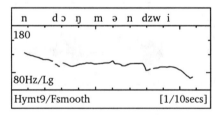

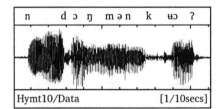

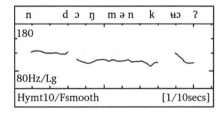

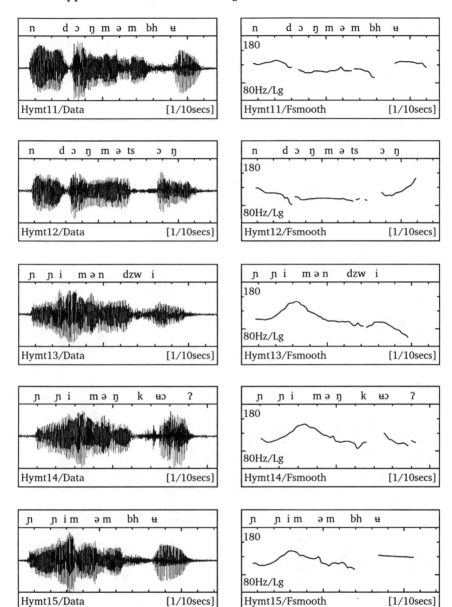

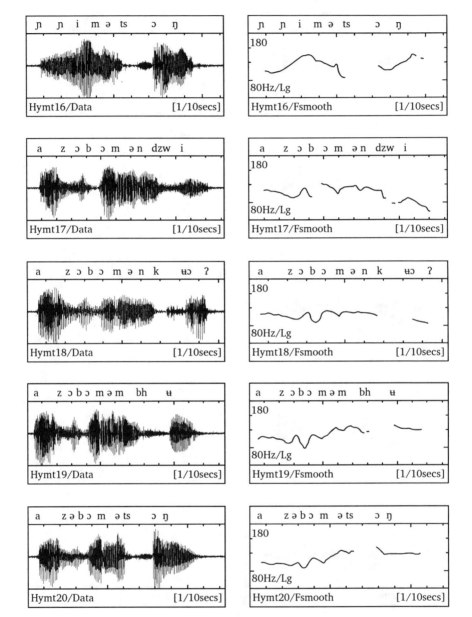

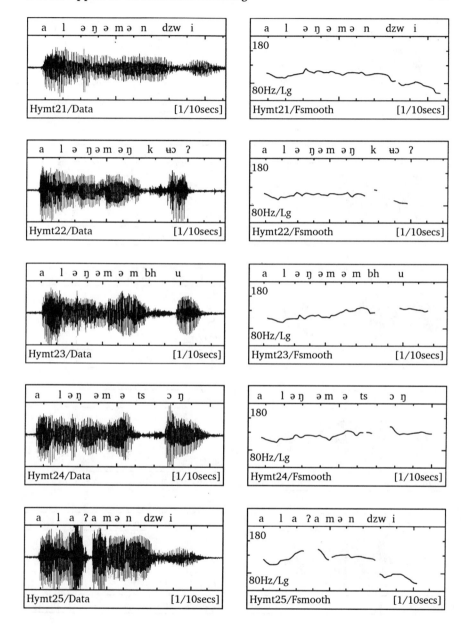

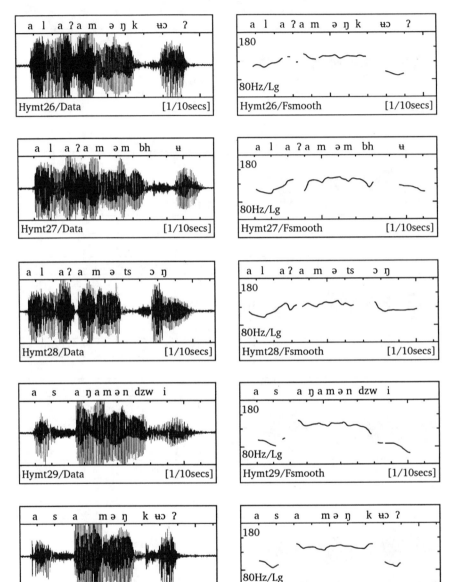

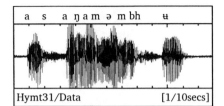

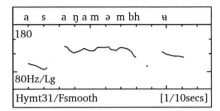

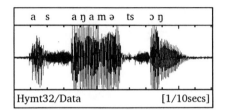

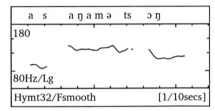

8

Critique of Selected Alternative Approaches

8.1 Clements (1983)[41]

The failure to account for the cumulative nature of register shift with models that employ binary features in the traditional manner, and the wish not to account for register shift with gradient features, have led to the development of some models that make use of hierarchical structures projected onto one geometric plane. Models that attempt to account for register shift with such structures include those of Clements (1981) (reprinted as Clements 1983), Clements (1990), and Huang (1980).

The fundamental insight common to these approaches is that the value of features that hierarchically dominate a given TBU is cumulative. In the case of Huang (1980) and Clements (1981, 1983), tonal features are arranged in hierarchical, branching tree structures not unlike the metrical trees used to account for stress assignment (cf. Liberman and Prince 1977).

Clements posits two features, "h" and "l," which correlate with "relatively high pitch" and "relatively low pitch," respectively. The features occupy tier-like "rows" which are geometrically arranged one above the other. Features from any given row may be associated with features from the row above

---

[41]This section is taken directly from §5.2 of Snider (1990a) and appears here with permission from the Linguistic Society of America. Other than a slight rewording of the text that pertains to example (160), it differs from the source only in matters of format; e.g., the example numbers and reference style have been changed in order to conform to the format style of the present work.

and with features from the row below. While a two-tone system would have only one row in underlying forms, a four-tone system would have two rows. An "unmarked" four-level system would thus receive the characterization of (158) (from Clements 1983:150), where A represents the highest tone and D the lowest.

(158)   row 1: h h l l
        row 2: h l h l
                ABCD

In order to account for the terracing effect of languages with downstep, hierarchical trees like that of (159) (Clements 1983:155) are constructed above the underlying tones according to language-specific algorithms.

(159)

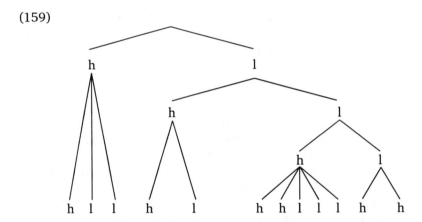

Phonetically, a structure such as (159) is interpreted hierarchically so that all features which dominate a given feature on the bottom row are grouped into "feature bundles," or matrices.

At the empirical level, while these hierarchical models are able to account for typical downstepping languages in an insightful manner, they are unable to account for languages like Krachi where a shift in register occurs between TBUs dominated by a single tone. The underlying form for the Krachi example in (160), for instance, would be characterized in Clements' model with the final *h* tone associated to the two final TBUs.

(160)

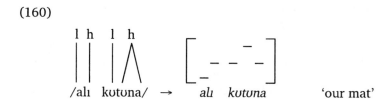

/alı kʊtʊna/ →   alı kʊtʊna   'our mat'

The problem for hierarchical models is inherent in the hierarchical concept itself: when a mother node dominates a daughter node, it also dominates all granddaughter nodes. If register shift is to be accounted for in the
manner demanded by these models, the shift must apply to all the TBUs
immediately dominated by the tone that has undergone the shift in register. In (160), regardless of how one constructs the tree above the tones,
whatever "happens" to the penultimate TBU will also "happen" to the final
TBU, since both are dominated by a single *h* tone. If more than one Hi tone
is involved, there would, of course, be no problem for these models, since
the TBUs that would undergo the shifts (up, followed by down, in the case
of Krachi) would each be associated with a separate Hi tone. But in Krachi
there is no reason to assume that more than one Hi tone is involved in
these cases.

In spite of inadequacies in accounting for languages like Krachi, the basic concept behind hierarchical monoplane models—the representation of
binary features in a manner which allows for a cumulative representation
of their values—is, I believe, essentially correct. What is needed for an ade-
quate analysis of Krachi and similar languages is a way of allowing
changes in tonal register to apply to specific TBUs, independently of the
tones associated with those TBUs. By recognizing two separate tonal tiers
that form different geometric planes with respect to a central tier, we are
able not only to capture the cumulative nature of register shifts, but also to
account for languages like Krachi.

8.2 Poser (1984), Beckman and Pierrehumbert (1986), and Pulleyblank (1986)

The register features *h* and *l*, as described above, are phonetically interpreted with a value relative to the preceding register setting. Because register
features are defined relatively, the present model is able to account for the cumulative nature of successive downsteps and upsteps in a principled manner.
Models that do not allow for the relative value of register features are unable
to account for the cumulative nature of successive downsteps and upsteps
with binary features. The tonal features *H* and *L* of RTT correspond well with

the tonal features [+/−High] of Yip (1980), renamed [+/−raised] in Pulleyblank (1986) and Yip (1993). The relatively defined register features *h* and *l*, however, differ significantly from the nonrelatively defined register features [+/−upper] of these proposals. The feature [upper] has a nonrelative value, i.e., it is either high or low. A model that employs [upper] then, serves well to differentiate phonemic tone levels, but it does not equate these levels with those produced by downstep or upstep.

In order to account for downstep, models that employ nonrelatively defined register features (e.g., Beckman and Pierrehumbert 1986, Pierrehumbert 1980, Pierrehumbert and Beckman 1988, Pulleyblank 1986) require the phonology component to output floating Lo tones to the phonetics (postbinary feature) component. These floating Lo's then trigger the phonetic pitch- implementation rules that are responsible for downstep. As Clark (1993) points out, this is a power that has probably never been claimed for nontonal features. One argument against allowing floating Lo tones to trigger downstep in the phonetics component concerns the advisability of allowing phonetic implementation rules to effect phonological differences. For many tonal languages, the presence versus the absence of nonautomatic downstep represents a phonological difference. Whether or not the phonetic downstep-implementation rules apply would therefore be phonologically significant. Since the application or nonapplication of *phonetic* implementation rules should never be *phonologically* significant, the case for assigning downstep to phonetic implementation rules is greatly weakened.

The register features employed in the phonetics components of the models in question have (nonbinary) scalar or gradient values, and are therefore very different from the binary phonological feature [Upper] these models use to distinguish phonemic tones. Accordingly, a number of arguments have been put forward against accounting for register shifts in the phonetics component (see Inkelas and Leben 1991, Ladd 1989, 1993 and Snider 1990a, 1998). Here is one of them.

In a number of languages that have three phonemic tone levels *and* the phenomenon of downstepped Hi, the downstepped Hi is described as being phonetically identical to the Mid. Languages like this include Supyire (Carlson 1983), Babanki (Hyman 1979), Moba (Russell 1996), and Kagoro (Van der Kolk 1992). Although the studies cited base their claims of phonetic equivalence on auditory impressions only, the number of languages and studies involved suggests that this type of equivalence is not coincidental. More recently, Snider (1998) reports on an instrumental study of downstep (both automatic and nonautomatic) in Bimoba, a three-tone Gur language spoken in Togo. In Bimoba, the lowering of the register that is attributable to downstep (both automatic and nonautomatic lower the register to the same degree) is equivalent to the difference in pitch between a

High tone and a following Mid tone. It is also the case that there is a similarity in phonological behavior between the downstepped Hi and the Mid in that both cause following Hi tones to be downstepped to their register. These facts argue strongly in favor of downstepped Hi's having the same phonological feature specification as Mid tones in Bimoba.

For those theories of tone that handle phonemic tonal differences with *phonological* features and register differences with separate *phonetic* features, there is no reason for the difference in pitch between a Hi and a downstepped Hi (a register difference) to be equal to that between a Hi and a Mid (a phonological difference). *Any* phonetic equivalence would be purely coincidental in these theories. On the other hand, if in undergoing downstep, a Hi tone assimilates to a preceding Lo in such a manner as to render the Hi *phonologically* identical to a Mid (i.e., so that it has the same feature representation as a Mid), the *phonetic* equivalence would not be coincidental. In these cases, the downstepped Hi and the Mid would both have the representation of Mid$_1$ (tonal feature H and register feature l).[42]

8.3 Hyman (1993)

In recent work on tonal geometry, Hyman (1993:79) criticizes models that employ the two-tier geometric structure advocated in this paper (he lists the models of Hyman 1986, Inkelas 1989, Leben et al. 1989, and Snider 1990a; and presumably would also include Hyman and Pulleyblank 1988, and Yip 1989, 1993) on the grounds that they are not able to adequately represent all of the relevant tonal distinctions found in natural language (i.e., they undergenerate). He argues that while the four heights distinguishable by these models adequately represent the maximum four *underlying* tone heights found in natural language, they are not able to account for the additional levels that are generated in certain *derived* contexts. In other words, in certain derived contexts one can find more than four levels of tone height that contrast with a given adjacent tone. Hyman's criticism of these models, however, is valid only for those models whose register features have a nonrelative interpretation (e.g., Hyman 1986, Hyman and Pulleyblank 1988, and Yip 1989). As discussed earlier, given the relative interpretation of the register features in the present

---

[42]This equivalence between downstepped Hi's and Mids does not obtain in all languages, however. Some descriptions of three-tone languages with downstep explicitly state that downstepped Hi's are phonetically higher than Mid tones. These include Armstrong (1968) and Newman (1971). In these cases I assume the Mid to have the representation of M$_2$ (tonal feature L and register feature h).

proposal, the model is able to represent up to six contrastive levels following any given tone.

As a solution to the problem of undergeneration, Hyman (1993) adopts the register and tonal tiers of the models he criticizes, but in addition he incorporates a third tier so that the model has one register tier and *two* tonal tiers. While his proposed solution probably does suffice to produce the relevant tonal distinctions found in natural languages, it also clearly over-generates since it allows for the representation of up to eight underlying level tones and a proliferation of contours. Moreover, given the register tier of his model, which is basically equivalent to that of the present proposal, Hyman's model would generate even more than eight levels (for the same reason that RTT can generate six levels as opposed to four levels). I am not aware of any languages that would require this much expressive power.

8.4 Clark (1993)

Like Hyman's (1993) proposal, Clark's (1993) proposal is similar in many respects to the present work. In Clark's model, the features [+/−UPPER], represented with upper case *H* and *L*, and the features [+/−RAISED], represented with lower case *h* and *l*, are linked to a tonal node which branches from the laryngeal node. The representation of *ɲí* in Bamileke-Dschang (Clark 1993:40) is shown in (161).

(161)   Representation of Hi tone in Clark (1993)

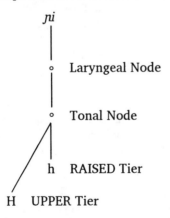

In Clark's model both features are *tonal*, and she criticizes models that employ register features to account for downstep. Instead, she claims that a phonetic interpretation rule like (162), where X is the "pitch standard," and "X_i and X_{i+1} are the values of X before and after register raising," reads directly off the phonological representation. This rule implements a downward adjustment of the pitch standard at the boundary of two adjacent identical features (e.g., *h h*) or identical tones (e.g., Mid Mid—tones being defined as a complex of features). Whether features or tones trigger the adjustment is language-specific. There is one important difference between the [UPPER] of Clark and the [upper] of others that employ the features [upper] and [raised]. While [UPPER] is a *tonal* feature in Clark's model, it is a *register* feature in both Pulleyblank's (1986) and Yip's (1993) models.

(162) $X_i \rightarrow X_{i+1}$ / [αT] _____ [αT]

In order to avoid clutter in the representations, Clark replaces the tonal nodes with a string of "phonemes," as in (163), but interprets such structures in a manner consistent with the geometry of (161).

(163)   Representation from Clark (1993:66)

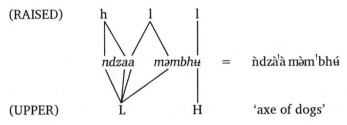

In (163), the sequences *h l* and *l l* both result in downstep at their junctures (although the former is not accounted for by the phonetic implementation rule in (162)). By way of contrast, the sequence *L H* (and in other examples *H L*) on the [UPPER] tier does not result in a change of register, making it clear that the two tiers do not function in the same way with respect to register. This undermines Clark's claim that a tier for register features is not needed.

(164)   Representation from Clark (1993:66)

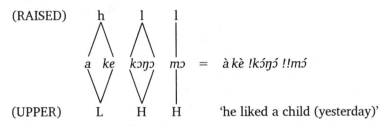

In (164), the [RAISED] features (lower case) are interpreted identically to those in (163). Also like (163), the sequence *L H* produces no change of register. Unlike (163), however, the sequence *H H* on the [UPPER] tier results in a further downstepping of the tonal register so that the TBU *mɔ́* is realized with a double downstep. Although Clark claims that there is no need of a register tier, her [RAISED] tier nevertheless functions in a manner very similar to the register tier of the present proposal. In both proposals, the sequences *h l* and *l l* result in downstep. So it is not clear what the advantages of her proposal are over those she criticizes. Furthermore, there are some problems.

One problem is that in accounting for register shifts by means of phonetic interpretation rules, there is no way to formally equate a downstepped Hi tone with a phonemic Mid tone in languages in which the two are phonetically equivalent. As discussed in §8.2, any equivalence between these two levels would be entirely coincidental in models that derive phonemic levels with phonological features and downstepped levels with phonetic interpretation rules.

Perhaps the greatest problem with Clark's proposal, however, lies in how it defines the OCP.

> I assume here that the Obligatory Contour Principle is not a universal convention, but a markedness condition which must be implemented by language-specific rules. In Dschang, the Obligatory Contour Principle is maintained, on the [UPPER] tier, throughout *most* [emphasis mine] of the phonology, but it is not maintained on the [RAISED] tier. (Clark 1993:42, fn 7)

This statement raises unanswered questions. In environments in which the OCP is maintained on the [UPPER] tier, why is it not also maintained on the [RAISED] tier? Also, what principled reason exists for why the OCP is maintained at certain times on the [UPPER] tier, but not maintained at other times? In (164), for example, there is only one [− UPPER] feature *L* associated to the two TBUs of *a ke*, but two [+UPPER] feature *Hs* associated to the three TBUs of *kɔŋɔ mɔ* in the same example. This only adds to the number of parameters in this model that need to be specified for each language. Summed up these include:

(a) which tiers the OCP applies to, and which tiers it does not apply to,
(b) when the OCP applies to any given tier, and when it does not,
(c) when a sequence of nonidentical features (e.g., *h l*) results in downstep, and when it does not (e.g., *H L*),
(d) whether a sequence of identical features (e.g. *h h*) results in downstep, or
(e) whether a sequence of identical tones (e.g., Mid Mid) results in downstep.

By way of contrast, these options do not exist for many models (including Register Tier Theory).

A final problem concerns how this model might account for upstep. Given that sequences of identical features always result in downstep, it is not clear how to account for upstep. One might expect that there would be an additional language specific parameter that would specify whether a sequence of identical features results in downstep, or whether it results in upstep.

8.5 Yip (1989, 1993)

Yip (1989, 1993) proposes a model in which the syllable (σ) dominates the tonal root node, which "is to be identified with the binary feature [upper]" (Yip 1989:169). The feature [upper] (a register feature) dominates the feature [raised] (a tonal feature), with *H* and *L* substituting as a shorthand for [+/− raised], respectively. This may be seen in the representation of a Hi-falling tone in (165).

(165)   Representation of Hi-falling tone in Yip (1989, 1993)

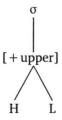

"Spreading of [raised] is thus independent of the specification for [upper], but spreading of [upper] automatically spreads the dependent value(s) for [raised] as well" (1989:169).

Given that Yip deals primarily with East Asian languages, it is not clear how the model would account for register phenomena in African languages. The first problem concerns the register feature [upper], and the second concerns the geometry assumed. Because the register features are not defined relatively, as they are in the present proposal, the model is open to the same criticisms raised above with respect to the other alternative approaches discussed; i.e., there is no way to formally equate downstepped phonetic levels with phonemic levels, and no way to account for terracing without recognizing unassociated, i.e., prosodically unlicensed, features in the phonetics component. Yip would probably agree. Following a discussion of Inkelas, Leben, and Cobler's (1987) treatment of register phenomena in Hausa, Yip (1993:262) concludes that the register features needed to account for terracing downstep in African languages "are not the same creature as the feature [upper] needed for East Asian languages." She bases this conclusion on the failure of [upper] to generate the successive lowerings of the tonal register that are needed in order to account for downstep, and also on the close association in African languages (apparently lacking in Asian languages) between [+upper] and [+raised], and between [−upper] and [−raised].

With respect to the feature geometry that Yip's model assumes, in spite of recognizing the need for [upper] and [register] to be able to spread independently even in Asian languages (see below), Yip (1993) continues the assumption of Yip (1989) that the register feature [upper] cannot spread independently of the melodic feature [raised]. Downstep in African languages, however, depends very much upon the independent spreading of register. In a language which has automatic downstep, a Hi tone that follows a Lo tone assimilates to the lower register (and only to the register) of the Lo tone. If spreading of the [−upper] register feature automatically includes the dependent value for [raised] as well, the result would be a complete assimilation, as in (166a), instead of the partial assimilation that is needed, as shown in (166b).

(166)   a.   b.

```
        σ        σ                        σ           σ
        |      .‡                         |           |
        | .·                              |           |
   [−upper]  [+upper]                  [−upper]   [+upper]
        |        |                         |       .‡
        |        |                         | .·
        L        H                         L           H
```

This problem can be overcome if one assumes that it is the dependent feature [raised] which corresponds to register in African languages. In (166b), the feature [−raised] (viz., L) is able to spread independently of [−upper] and correctly generates the partial assimilation that is needed to account for automatic downstep. But this assumption leads to a further problem.

If [raised], which is dominated by [upper], is now a register feature, it is not possible for two TBUs that are associated to the same feature [upper] to be realized on different registers (e.g., two TBUs associated to a single Hi tone could never be realized with the surface sequence Hi'Hi). This is demonstrated in (167a) and (167b), neither of which is satisfactory.

(167)   a.   b.

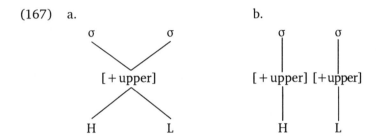

In (167a), when H and L, now register features, are associated to [+upper], now a tonal feature, the result is a falling contour tone associated to two TBUs, as opposed to a sequence Hi'Hi. While (167b) would produce the desired surface result (viz., Hi'Hi), the two TBUs are not associated to a single feature [+upper]. This is needed, however, in some languages, as demonstrated for Krachi in Snider (1990a).

Yip is aware of problems like this and admits the need for register and melody to spread independently even in Asian languages.

> There is a technical problem here in the feature geometry argued for in Yip (1989). If the H, L tones are dependents of [upper], spreading of upper should carry the dependent tones along with it, and yet this is exactly what does not happen in Fuzhou, where the first syllables keeps its LH rise....A better model for these facts would be Shih (1986:22), in which register and melody are sister nodes which can each spread independently. (Yip 1993:248, fn 5)

I, therefore, conclude (perhaps with Yip, herself) that Yip (1989, 1993) does not provide a satisfactory account of register phenomena in African languages.

References

Anderson, Stephen R. 1978. Tone features. In Victoria A. Fromkin (ed.), Tone: A linguistic survey, 133–75. New York: Academic Press.

Archangeli, Diana. 1988. Aspects of underspecification theory. Phonology 5(2):183-207.

———— and Douglas Pulleyblank. 1994. Grounded phonology. Cambridge, Mass: MIT Press.

Armstrong, Robert. 1968. Yala (Ikom): A terraced-level language with three tones. The Journal of West African Languages 5(1):49–58.

Beckman, Mary and Janet Pierrehumbert. 1986. Intonational structure in Japanese and English. Phonology Yearbook 3:255–309.

Bird, Steven and Oliver Stegen. 1995. The Bamileke Dschang associative construction: Instrumental findings. Technical report RP66. Edinburgh: Centre for Cognitive Science, University of Edinburgh.

Carlson, Robert. 1983. Downstep in Supyire. Studies in African Linguistics 14(1):35–45.

Casali, Roderic F. 1994. Nominal tone in Nawuri. Journal of West African Languages 24(2):45–64.

Chan, Marjorie K. M. 1991. Contour tone spreading and tone sandhi in Danyang Chinese. Phonology 8(2):237–59.

Clark, Mary. 1988. An accentual analysis of the Zulu noun. In Harry Van der Hulst and Norval Smith (eds.), Autosegmental studies on pitch accent, 51–79. Dordrecht: Foris Publications.

————. 1993. Representation of downstep in Dschang Bamileke. In Harry Van der Hulst and Keith Snider (eds.), 29–73.

161

Clements, George N. 1981. The hierarchical representation of tone. In
    George N. Clements (ed.), Harvard studies in phonology 2, 108–77.
    Cambridge, Mass.: Harvard University Linguistics Department.

———. 1983. The hierarchical representation of tone features. In I.
    Dihoff (ed.), Current approaches to African linguistics, vol. 1,
    145–76. Dordrecht: Foris Publications.

———. 1985. The geometry of phonological features. Phonology Year-
    book 2:223–52.

———. 1989. A unified set of features for consonants and vowels. Cornell
    University. ms.

———. 1990. The status of register in intonation theory: Comments on
    the papers by Ladd and by Inkelas and Leben. In Mary E. Beckman
    and John Kingston (eds.), Laboratory Phonology 1, 58–71. Cam-
    bridge: Cambridge University Press.

———. 1996. Review of "The phonology of tone: The representation of
    tonal register, edited by Harry Van der Hulst and Keith Snider."
    Language 72(4):847–52.

——— and Elizabeth V. Hume. 1995. The internal organization of speech
    sounds. In John A. Goldsmith (ed.), The handbook of phonological
    theory, 245–306. Oxford: Blackwell Publishers.

Connell, Bruce. 1994. The structure of labial-velar stops. Journal of
    Phonetics 22(4):441–76.

——— and D. Robert Ladd. 1990. Aspects of pitch realisation in Yoruba.
    Phonology 7(1):1–29.

Elugbe, Ben O. 1986. The analysis of falling tones in Ghotuo. In Koen
    Bogers, Harry Van der Hulst, and Maarten Mous (eds.), The phono-
    logical representation of suprasegmentals, 51–62. Dordrecht: Foris.

Flik, Eva. 1977. Tone glides and registers in five Dan dialects. Linguistics
    201:5–59.

Goldsmith, John. 1976. Autosegmental phonology. Ph.D. dissertation.
    Massachusetts Institute of Technology, Cambridge.

———. 1984. Meeussen's rule. In Mark Aronoff and Richard T. Oehrle
    (eds.), Language sound structure, 245–59. Cambridge, Mass.: MIT Press.

———. 1990 Autosegmental and metrical phonology. Oxford: Basil
    Blackwell.

Halle, Morris. 1992. Phonological features. In W. Bright (ed.), International
    encyclopedia of linguistics, vol. 3, 207–12. Oxford: Oxford University
    Press.

Huang, Cheng-Teh James. 1980. The metrical structure of terraced-level
    tones. Proceedings of North Eastern Linguistic Society 10, Cahiers
    linguistiques d'Ottawa 9:257–70.

Hyman, Larry M. 1979. Tonology of the Babanki noun. Studies in African Linguistics 10(2):159–77.

———. 1985. Word domains and downstep in Bamileke-Dschang. Phonology Yearbook 2:85–138.

———. 1986. The representation of multiple tone heights. In Koen Bogers, Harry Van der Hulst, and Maarten Mous (eds.), The phonological representation of suprasegmentals, 109–52. Dordrecht: Foris.

———. 1992. Moraic mismatches in Bantu. Phonology 9(2):255–65.

———. 1993. Register tones and tonal geometry. In Harry Van der Hulst and Keith Snider (eds.), 75–108.

——— and Douglas Pulleyblank. 1988. On feature copying: Parameters of tone rules. In Larry M. Hyman and Charles N. Li (eds.), Language, speech and mind: Studies in honour of Victoria A. Fromkin, 30–47. Kent: Croom Helm.

——— and Maurice Tadadjeu. 1976. Floating tones in Mbam-Nkam. In Larry Hyman (ed.), Studies in Bantu tonology, 57–111. Southern California Occasional Papers in Linguistics 3. Los Angeles: University of Southern California.

Inkelas, Sharon. 1987. Tone feature geometry. In James Blevins and Julie Carter (eds.), Proceedings of North Eastern Linguistic Society 18, 223–37. Amherst, Mass.: GLSA.

———. 1989. Register tone and the phonological representation of downstep. In Laurice Tuller and Isabelle Haik (eds.), Current approaches to African linguistics 6, 65–82. Dordrecht: Foris.

——— and William R. Leben. 1991. Where phonology and phonetics intersect: the case of Hausa intonation. In John Kingston and Mary E. Beckman (eds.), Papers in laboratory phonology 1: Between the grammar and physics of speech, 17–35. Cambridge: Cambridge University Press.

———, William R. Leben and Mark Cobler. 1987. The phonology of intonation in Hausa. In James Blevins and Julie Carter (eds.), Proceedings of North Eastern Linguistic Society 17, 327–42. Amherst, Mass: GLSA.

Itô, Junko. 1986. Syllable theory in prosodic phonology. Ph.D. dissertation. Massachusetts Institute of Technology, Cambridge.

Katamba, Francis. 1989. An introduction to phonology. London: Longman Group UK.

Kenstowicz, Michael. 1994. Phonology in generative grammar. Oxford: Blackwell.

Kiparsky, Paul. 1982a. Lexical phonology and morphology. In I. S. Yang (ed.), Linguistics in the morning calm, 3–91. Seoul: Hanshin.

————. 1982b. From cyclic to lexical phonology. In Harry Van der Hulst and Norval Smith (eds.), The structure of phonological representations, part 1, 131-75. Dordrecht: Foris.

————. 1985. Some consequences of lexical phonology. Phonology Yearbook 2:83–138.

Ladd, Robert 1984. Declination: A review and some hypotheses. Phonology Yearbook 1:53–74.

————. 1989. Review of Pierrehumbert and Beckman 1988. Journal of Linguistics 25:519–26.

————. 1993. In defense of a metrical theory of intonational downstep. In Harry Van der Hulst and Keith Snider (eds.), 109–32.

Leben, William R. 1971. Suprasegmental and segmental representation of tone. Studies in African Linguistics, Supplement 2:183–200.

————. 1973. Suprasegmental phonology. Ph.D. dissertation. Massachusetts Institute of Technology, Cambridge.

————. 1978. The representation of tone. In Victoria Fromkin (ed.), Tone: A linguistic survey, 177–219. New York: Academic Press.

————, Sharon Inkelas, and Mark Cobler. 1989. Phrases and phrase tones in Hausa. In Paul Newman and Robert D. Botne (eds.), Current approaches to African linguistics, 5, 45-61. Dordrecht: Foris.

Leroy, Jacqueline. 1977. Morphologie et classes nominales en Mankon (Cameroun). Paris: Société d´Études Linguistiques et Anthropologiques de France (SELAF).

Liberman, Mark and Alan Prince. 1977. On stress and linguistic rhythm. Linguistic Inquiry 8:249–336.

Longacre, Robert E. 1952. Five phonemic pitch levels in Trique. Acta Linguistica 7:62–82.

McCarthy, John. 1986. OCP effects: Gemination and antigemination. Linguistic Inquiry 17:207–63.

Mfonyam, Joseph Ngwa. 1988. Tone in orthography: The case of Bafut. Doctoral dissertation. The University of Yaoundé, Yaoundé, Cameroon.

Mohanan, Karavannur P. 1982. The theory of lexical phonology. Ph.D. dissertation. Massachusetts Institute of Technology, Cambridge.

————. 1986. The theory of lexical phonology. Dordrecht: D. Reidel.

Myers, Scott. 1995. The phonological word in Shona. In Francis Katamba (ed.), Bantu phonology and morphology, 69–92. München, Germany: Lincom Europa.

Newman, Roxana M. 1971. Downstep in Ga'anda. Journal of African Linguistics 10(1):15–27.

Odden, David. 1980. Associative tone in Shona. Journal of Linguistic Research 1(2):37–51.

————. 1986. On the obligatory contour principle. Language 62(2):353–83.

References 165

————. 1988a. Anti-antigemination and the OCP. Linguistic Inquiry 19:451–75.

————. 1988b. predictable tone systems in Bantu. In Harry Van der Hulst and Norval Smith, (eds.), Autosegmental studies on pitch accent, 225–51. Dordrecht: Foris.

————. 1996. The phonology and morphology of Kimatuumbi. Oxford: Clarendon.

Paulian, Christiane. 1974. Le kukuya: Langue teke du Congo. Paris: Société d'Etudes Linguistiques et Anthropologiques de France (CNRS).

Pierrehumbert, Janet. 1980. The phonology and phonetics of English intonation. Ph.D. dissertation, Massachusetts Institute of Technology, Cambridge.

———— and Mary Beckman. 1988. Japanese tone structure. Cambridge, Mass.: MIT Press.

Pike, Eunice and Kent Wistrand. 1974. Step-up terrace tone in Acatlán Mixtec (Mexico). In Ruth M. Brend (ed.), Advances in tagmemics, 81–104. Amsterdam: North Holland.

Poser, William. 1984. The phonetics and phonology of tone and intonation in Japanese. Ph.D. dissertation. Massachusetts Institute of Technology, Cambridge.

Pulleyblank, Douglas. 1986. Tone in lexical phonology. Dordrecht: D. Reidel.

Russell, Jann. 1996. Some tonal sandhi rules in Moba. Summer Institute of Linguistics, Togo. ms.

Schane, Sanford A. 1995. Diphthongization in particle phonology. In John A. Goldsmith (ed.), The handbook of phonological theory, 586–608. Oxford: Blackwell.

Shih, Chi-Lin. 1986. The prosodic domain of tone sandhi in Chinese. Ph.D. dissertation. University of California at San Diego.

Snider, Keith L. 1986. Apocope, tone, and the glottal stop in Chumburung. Journal of African Languages and Linguistics 8(2):133–44.

————. 1988. Towards the representation of tone: A three-dimensional approach. In Harry Van der Hulst and Norval Smith (eds.), Features, segmental structure and harmony processes, part 1, 237–65. Dordrecht: Foris.

————. 1989. Vowel coalescence in Chumburung: An autosegmental analysis. Lingua 78:217–32.

————. 1990a. Tonal upstep in Krachi: Evidence for a register tier. Language 66(3):453–74.

————. 1990b. Studies in Guang phonology. D.Litt. dissertation. University of Leiden, Leiden, The Netherlands.

———. 1990c. Tone in proto-Guang nouns. African Languages and Cultures 3(1):87–107.

———. 1998. Phonetic realisation of downstep in Bimoba. Phonology 15(1):77–101.

———. 1999. Tonal "upstep" in Engenni. The Journal of West African Languages 27(1).

Stahlke, Herbert. 1971. Topics in Ewe phonology. Ph.D. dissertation. University of California at Los Angeles.

Stevens, Kenneth N. and Samuel J. Keyser. 1989. Primary features and their enhancement in consonants. Language 65(1):81–106.

———, Samuel J. Keyser, and Haruko Kawasaki. 1986. Toward a phonetic and phonological theory of redundant features. In Joseph S. Perkell and Dennis H. Klatt (eds.), Invariance and variability in speech processes, 426–49. Hillsdale, N.J.: Lawrence Erlbaum Associates.

Stewart, John M. 1965. The typology of the Twi tone system. Preprint from the Bulletin of the Institute of African Studies 1, Institute of African Studies, University of Ghana, Legon, Ghana.

———. 1983. Downstep and floating low tones in Adioukrou. Journal of African Languages and Linguistics 5(1):57–78.

——— and Hélène Van Leynseele. 1979. Underlying cross-height vowel harmony in Nen (Bantu A.44). Journal of African Languages and Linguistics 1(1):31–54.

Tadadjeu, Maurice. 1974. Floating tones, shifting rules, and downstep in Dschang-Bamileke. Studies in African Linguistics, Supplement 5:283–90.

Thomas, Elaine. 1974. Engenni. In John Bendor-Samuel (ed.), Studies in Nigerian languages 4, ten Nigerian tone systems, 13–26. Kano, Nigeria: Institute of Linguistics, Jos, and Centre for the Study of Nigerian Languages, Abdullahi Bayero College, Ahmadu Bello University.

———. 1978. A grammatical description of the Engenni language. Summer Institute of Linguistics and University of Texas at Arlington Publications in Linguistics 60. Dallas.

Van der Hulst, Harry and Keith Snider, eds. 1993. The phonology of tone: the representation of tonal register. Berlin: Mouton de Gruyter.

Van der Kolk, Kees. 1992. The three-level terraced tone system of Kagoro. Ph.D. thesis. University of Leiden, Leiden, The Netherlands.

Wang, William. 1967. Phonological Features of Tone. International Journal of American Linguistics 33(2):93–105.

Watters, John. 1997. Tone in western Ejagham (Etung). Summer Institute of Linguistics, Cameroon. ms.

Woo, Nancy. 1969. Prosody and phonology. Ph.D. dissertation. Massachusetts Institute of Technology, Cambridge.

Yip, Moira. 1980. The tonal phonology of Chinese. Ph.D. dissertation. Massachusetts Institute of Technology, Cambridge.

———. 1989. Contour tones. Phonology 6(1):149–74.

———. 1993. Tonal register in East Asian languages. In Harry Van der Hulst and Keith Snider (eds.), 245–68.

Zsiga, Elizabeth C. 1992. A mismatch between morphological and prosodic domains: Evidence from two Igbo rules. Phonology 9(1):101–35.

Index

Summer Institute of Linguistics and
The University of Texas at Arlington
Publications in Linguistics

Recent Publications

133. **The geometry and features of tone,** by Keith Snider. 1999.
132. **Desano Grammar: Studies in the languages of Colombia 6,** by Marion Miller. 1999.
131. **The structure of evidential categories in Wanka Quechua,** by Rick Floyd. 1999.
130. **Cubeo grammar: Studies in the languages of Colombia 5,** by Nancy L. Morse and Michael B. Maxwell. 1999.
129. **Aspects of Zaiwa prosody: An autosegmental account,** by Mark W. Wannemacher. 1998.
128. **Tense and aspect in Obolo grammar and discourse,** by Uche Aaron. 1998.
127. **Case grammar applied,** by Walter A. Cook, S.J. 1998.
126. **The Dong language in Guizhou Province, China,** by Long Yaohong and Zheng Guoqiao, translated from Chinese by D. Norman Geary. 1998.
125. **Vietnamese classifiers in narrative texts,** by Karen Ann Daley. 1998.
124. **Comparative Kadai: The Tai branch,** ed. by Jerold A. Edmondson and David B. Solnit. 1997.
123. **Why there are no clitics: An alternative perspective on pronominal allomorphy,** by Daniel L. Everett. 1996.
122. **Mamaindé stress: The need for strata,** by David Eberhard. 1995.
121. **The Doyayo language: Selected studies,** by Elisabeth Wiering and Marinus Wiering. 1994.
120. **A discourse analysis of First Corinthians,** by Ralph Bruce Terry. 1995.
119. **Discourse features of ten languages of West-Central Africa,** ed. by Stephen H. Levensohn. 1994.
118. **Epena Pedee syntax: Studies in the languages of Colombia 4,** by Phillip Lee Harms. 1994.
117. **Beyond the bilingual classroom: Literacy acquisition among Peruvian Amazon communities,** by Barbara Trudell. 1993.
116. **The French imparfait and passé simple in discourse,** by Sharon Rebecca Rand. 1993.

93. **Development and diversity: Language variation across time and space (A Festschrift for Charles-James N. Bailey),** ed. by Jerold A. Edmondson, Crawford Feagin, and Peter Mühlhäusler. 1990.

92. **Comanche dictionary and grammar,** ed. by Lila W. Robinson and James Armagost. 1990.

91. **Language maintenance in Melanesia: Sociolinguistics and social networks in New Caledonia,** by Stephen J. Schooling. 1990.

90. **Studies in the syntax of Mixtecan languages 2,** ed. by C. Henry Bradley and Barbara E. Hollenbach. 1990.

89. **Comaltepec Chinantec syntax: Studies in Chinantec languages 3,** by Judi Lynn Anderson. 1989.

88. **Lealao Chinantec syntax: Studies in Chinantec languages 2,** by James E. Rupp. 1989.

87. **An etymological dictionary of the Chinantec languages: Studies in Chinantec languages 1,** by Calvin R. Rensch. 1989.

86. **Comparative Kadai: Linguistic studies beyond Tai,** ed. by Jerold A. Edmondson and David B. Solnit. 1988.

85. **The verbal piece in Ebira,** by John R. Adive. 1989.

84. **Insights into Tagalog: Reduplication, infixation, and stress from nonlinear phonology,** by Koleen M. French. 1988.

83. **Studies in the syntax of Mixtecan languages 1,** ed. by C. Henry Bradley and Barbara E. Hollenbach. 1988.

82. **Dinka vowel system,** by Job Malou. 1988.

81. **Aspects of Western Subanon formal speech,** by William C. Hall. 1987.

80. **Current trends and issues in Hispanic linguistics,** ed. by Lenard Studerus. 1987.

79. **Modes in Dényá discourse,** by Samson Negbo Abangma. 1987.

78. **Tense/aspect and the development of auxiliaries in Kru languages,** by Lynelle Marchese. 1986.

77. **Discourse features of Korean narration,** by Shin Ja Joo Hwang. 1987.

76. **Hixkaryana and linguistic typology,** by Desmond C. Derbyshire. 1985.

75. **Sentence initial devices,** ed. by Joseph E. Grimes. 1986.

74. **English phonetic transcription,** by Charles-James N. Bailey. 1985.

73. **Pragmatics in non-Western perspective,** ed. by George Huttar and Kenneth J. Gregerson. 1986.

72. **Senoufo phonology, discourse to syllable (a prosodic approach),** by Elizabeth Mills. 1984.

53. **Grammatical analysis,** by Kenneth L. Pike and Evelyn G. Pike. 1977.

52.3. **Discourse grammar: Studies in indigenous languages of Colombia, Panama, and Ecuador 3,** ed. by Robert E. Longacre and Frances Woods. 1977.

52.2. **Discourse grammar: Studies in indigenous languages of Colombia, Panama, and Ecuador 2,** ed. by Robert E. Longacre and Frances Woods. 1977.

52.1. **Discourse grammar: Studies in indigenous languages of Colombia, Panama, and Ecuador 1,** ed. by Robert E. Longacre and Frances Woods. 1976.

51. **Papers on discourse,** ed. by Joseph E. Grimes. 1978.

For further information or a full listing of SIL publications contact:

International Academic Bookstore
Summer Institute of Linguistics
7500 W. Camp Wisdom Road
Dallas, TX 75236-5699

Voice: 972-708-7404
Fax: 972-708-7433
Email: academic.books@sil.org
Internet: http://www.sil.org